CYCLE A

BUILDING FAMILY FAITH

LISA M. BELLECCI-ST.ROMAIN

LIGUORI
PUBLICATIONS
ONE LIGUORI DRIVE
LIGUORI, MO 63057-9999
(314) 464-2500

Imprimi Potest:
James Shea, C.SS.R.
Provincial, St. Louis Province
The Redemptorists

Imprimatur:
+ Edward J. O'Donnell, D.D.
Archdiocesan Administrator, Archdiocese of St. Louis

ISBN 0-89243-542-9
Library of Congress Catalog Card Number: 93-79278

Cover and interior art by Chris Sharp

YEAR A

Page	Sunday or Feast	1995	1998	2001
9	1st. Sun. Advent	3 Dec.	29 Nov.	2 Dec.
9	2nd Sun. Advent	10 Dec.	6 Dec.	9 Dec.
11	3rd Sun. Advent	17 Dec.	13 Dec.	16 Dec.
12	4th Sun. Advent	24 Dec.	20 Dec.	23 Dec.
17	Holy Family	31 Dec.	27 Dec.	30 Dec.

Page	Sunday or Feast	1996	1999	2002
18	2nd Sun. After Christmas	7 Jan.	3 Jan.	6 Jan.
19	Epiphany	7 Jan.	3 Jan.	6 Jan.
20	Baptism of Lord	—	10 Jan.	13 Jan.
25	2nd Ord. Sun.	14 Jan.	17 Jan.	20 Jan.
26	3rd Ord. Sun.	21 Jan.	24 Jan.	27 Jan.
27	4th Ord. Sun.	28 Jan.	31 Jan.	3 Feb.
28	5th Ord. Sun.	4 Feb.	7 Feb.	10 Feb.
29	6th Ord. Sun.	11 Feb.	14 Feb.	—
30	7th Ord. Sun.	18 Feb.	—	—
31	8th Ord. Sun.	-	—	—
32	9th Ord. Sun.	—	—	—
33	Trinity Sun.	2 June	30 May	26 May
34	Body and Blood	9 June	6 June	2 June
35	10th Ord. Sun.	—	—	9 June
36	11th Ord. Sun.	16 June	13 June	16 June
37	12th Ord. Sun.	23 June	20 June	23 June
38	13th Ord. Sun.	30 June	27 June	30 June
39	14th Ord. Sun.	7 July	4 July	7 July
41	15th Ord. Sun.	14 July	11 July	14 July
42	16th Ord. Sun.	21 July	18 July	21 July
43	17th Ord. Sun.	28 July	25 July	28 July
44	18th Ord. Sun.	4 Aug.	1 Aug.	4 Aug.
45	19th Ord. Sun.	11 Aug.	8 Aug.	11 Aug.
46	Assumption	—	15 Aug.	—
47	20th Ord. Sun.	18 Aug.	-	18 Aug.
48	21st Ord. Sun.	25 Aug.	22 Aug.	25 Aug.

Page	Sunday or Feast	1996	1999	2002
49	22nd Ord. Sun.	1 Sept.	29 Aug.	1 Sept.
50	23rd Ord. Sun.	8 Sept.	5 Sept.	8 Sept.
52	24th Ord. Sun.	15 Sept.	12 Sept.	15 Sept.
53	25th Ord. Sun.	22 Sept.	19 Sept.	22 Sept.
54	26th Ord. Sun.	29 Sept.	26 Sept.	29 Sept.
55	27th Ord. Sun.	6 Oct.	3 Oct.	6 Oct.
57	28th Ord. Sun.	13 Oct.	10 Oct.	13 Oct.
58	29th Ord. Sun.	20 Oct.	17 Oct.	20 Oct.
59	30th Ord. Sun.	27 Oct.	24 Oct.	27 Oct.
60	31st Ord. Sun.	3 Nov.	31 Oct.	3 Nov.
61	32nd Ord. Sun.	10 Nov.	7 Nov.	10 Nov.
62	33rd Ord. Sun.	17 Nov.	14 Nov.	17 Nov.
64	Christ the King	24 Nov.	21 Nov.	24 Nov.
69	1st Sun. of Lent	25 Feb.	21 Feb.	17 Feb.
70	2nd Sun. of Lent	3 Mar.	28 Feb.	24 Feb.
70	3rd Sun. of Lent	10 Mar.	7 Mar.	3 Mar.
72	4th Sun. of Lent	17 Mar.	14 Mar.	10 Mar.
73	5th Sun. of Lent	24 Mar.	21 Mar.	17 Mar.
74	Passion Sun.	31 Mar.	28 Mar.	24 Mar.
79	Easter Sun.	7 Apr.	4 Apr.	31 Mar.
80	2nd Sun. Easter	14 Apr.	11 Apr.	7 Apr.
81	3rd Sun. Easter	21 Apr.	18 Apr.	14 Apr.
83	4th Sun. Easter	28 Apr.	25 Apr.	21 Apr.
84	5th Sun. Easter	5 May	2 May	28 Apr.
85	6th Sun. Easter	12 May	9 May	5 May
86	7th Sun. Easter	19 May	16 May	12 May
87	Pentecost Sun.	26 May	23 May	19 May

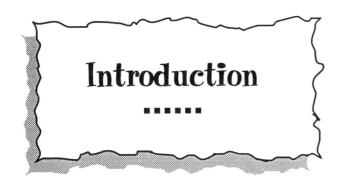

Introduction

- - - - - -

HAVE YOU WISHED for a book that could help you share your faith with your children, a book that does not bore them or become tedious for you?

This book is that book! It gives your family a chance to share and think, while having fun with one another. As a family, you can study the Sunday Scriptures to make them come alive for your children. (Some weeks cite only a portion of the entire reading.) How you use the questions for reflection depends on the ages of your children or their desire to consider the issues. Use your judgment; see what works each week and what feels complete.

Each session is designed to last about fifteen minutes, but there might be times when a good discussion keeps the session going longer. Some sessions require additional time and effort on the part of the leader.

All sessions end with a "treat" (suggestions provided). Sugar-free dietary needs have been considered, and many suggestions are available in both sugar and nonsugar forms. If you don't find the treat appropriate, choose something else. Enjoy your treat around the table or in the family meeting place to reinforce a sense of family unity.

The items needed for each session are generally those found around the house; options, however, are provided. The leader has the responsibility of gathering the items for his or her week and making any necessary advance preparations. Note: the leader need not always be a parent in the household. Grandparents or other relatives might like a turn, and older children can benefit from leading something fun, yet Scripture-oriented. The leader, however, should be old enough to take precautions around young children when materials and activities call for safety.

Set aside one special place in your house for your family's altar. It could be a corner table, the top of the television, the middle of the kitchen or dining-room table—anywhere your family decides. Each week the text will suggest placing something on the family altar space for the week. Thus, the space should not inconvenience family routine.

As an additional way to help your children connect what happens at home with what happens in church, get a yard of material the color of the liturgical season and drape it across the altar space. (See Appendix A on page 91 for the listing of colors and seasons.) When the family gathers for the next session, remove the items on the altar to make room for the ones suggested for that week. Note: If candles are used, be sure to extinguish them at the end of each session.

To accommodate family schedules, it's important to set aside a regular time to gather the family. Some families prefer to gather before Sunday liturgy to have an idea of what's coming up at church. Others gather the following week, to continue what they heard at church on Sunday. You decide what fits your family's schedule and preferences. With weekly regularity, growth and good times are guaranteed!

THE SEASON OF
ADVENT

First Sunday of Advent

......

Theme: All people shall seek God.

Reading:
Isaiah 2:2-5
(Reading I)
In days to come, the mountain of the Lord's house shall be established as the highest mountain and raised above the hills. All nations shall stream toward it; many peoples shall come and say: "Come, let us climb the mountain of God, that we may be instructed in God's ways and walk in God's paths." For from Zion shall go forth instruction, and the word of God from Jerusalem. And God shall judge between the nations and impose terms on many people. They shall beat their swords into plowshares and their spears into pruning hooks; one nation shall not raise the sword against another, nor shall they train for war again. Come, let us walk in the light of God!

Materials: ✓ magazines ✓ newspapers ✓ small poster board or piece of construction paper (cut into the shape of a mountain) ✓ glue ✓ scissors ✓ Advent candles (optional)

Treat: mixed nuts (If this is not available, share any other treat you might have.)

Leader's Instructions: Gather the family, open with prayer, and read the Scripture. Have each family member cut from the magazines and newspapers three pictures or articles of people who are different in nationality, culture, age, and so forth. Glue these to the poster board or construction paper that is cut in the shape of a mountain. Lead the Share and Commit sections.

Share: God wants all people, including these people, to share in everlasting life. How does if feel to imagine that? Who are the people you find most difficult to accept? Why? Is the "path" you are on now helping to change this? Might there be something you need to change, either the way you treat others, the way you think about them, or how you feel toward them in your heart? What "sword" (destructive feeling or action) do you need to make into a "plowshare" (constructive feeling or action)?

Commit: This week let's try hard, asking for God's help, to change our hearts so that we're more accepting of those who are different.

Altar Sign: Place on the altar space the poster or paper collage your family has made as a reminder of the variety of people who are invited to be with God forever.

Prayer: Dear God, creator of all people, we pray for the grace to accept each person in our hearts. We pray that all people may come to know you and walk in your light. We pray for peace in our world. Amen.

Close: Share a hug, and then enjoy the treat.

Second Sunday of Advent

......

Theme: We must reform our lives.

Reading:
Matthew 3:1-6, 9-10
(Gospel)
When John the Baptist made his appearance as a preacher in the desert of Judea, this was his theme: "Reform your lives! The reign of God

is at hand." It was of him that the prophet Isaiah had spoken: "A herald's voice in the desert: 'Prepare the way of the Lord, make straight his paths.'" John was clothed in a garment of camel's hair and wore a leather belt around his waist. Grasshoppers and wild honey were his food. At that time, Jerusalem, all Judea, and the whole region around the Jordan were going out to him. They were being baptized by him in the Jordan River as they confessed sins. John said, "Do not pride yourselves on the claim, 'We are children of Abraham and Sarah.' God can raise up children to Abraham and Sarah from these very stones! Even now the ax is laid to the root of the tree. Every tree that is not fruitful will be cut down and thrown into the fire."

Materials: ✓ pieces of string (10 to 12 inches long, one per person) ✓ a branch from a tree (See Leader's Instructions.) ✓ Advent candles (optional)

Treat: honey on crackers

Leader's Instructions: The family can choose one of three ways to cut a branch of a tree: (1) Go outside together and cut an unwanted plant or tree, or even a small limb of a tree. (2) Many families get Christmas trees around this time. Cut off the dry or unwanted branches. (3) Chop down your own tree, connecting the symbol of evergreen to reforming your lives to live forever with Christ. Place the branch within the family circle, and open with prayer. Read the Scripture, and lead the Share and Commit sections.

Share: Though many people are preparing for Christmas and getting excited about presents, we are asked to get very serious this week as we think about confessing sins and making ourselves ready for the coming of the Lord.

If Jesus were to come and live with us here in our house, what are some things you might want to do to get ready? In what ways are you a "fruitful" tree now? What things in your life do you need to reform at home? at school? at work? with friends? How can you remember that Jesus is with you as you work on things you want to reform? How can our family help you remember?

Pick one thing you would like to change as you prepare for Jesus to live with you. Take a string and tie it to one of the branches as a sign that you want to remember to think of Jesus' encouragement.

Commit: This week, let's try to reform our lives in some way, no matter how small.

Altar Sign: Lay the branch with strings tied to it on the altar space to remind the family of their desire to reform.

Prayer: Dear God, you always want the best for us. We want to be ready for you; we want to be ready to receive Jesus in a new way at Christmastime. We pray for the grace to be faithful to our commitments this week. Amen.

Close: Share a hug, and think of the John the Baptist as you enjoy your treat.

Third Sunday of Advent

······

Theme: We must share God's favor with others.

Reading: *Matthew 11:2-6 (Gospel)*
John in prison heard about the works Christ performed and sent a message through his disciples to ask him, "Are you 'he who is to come' or do we look for another?" In reply, Jesus said to them: "Go back and report to John what you hear and see: the blind recover their sight, cripples walk, lepers are cured, the deaf hear, the dead are raised to life, and the poor have the good news preached to them. Blest is the one who finds no stumbling block in me."

Materials: ✓ earplugs or blindfolds for each person ✓ Advent candles (optional)

Treat: a "grab bag" (Put a variety of candies, dried fruit, pretzels, or whatever you have available in a paper bag. Each person will pull a "treat" from the bag without looking.)

Leader's Instructions: Fifteen or twenty minutes before the family gathers, have each person put on a piece of "handicapping apparatus." Encourage everyone to continue in his or her routine until meeting time. (Leader, you should do the same. Use a timer if you are blindfolded.)

After the time is up, invite everyone to gather at the meeting area. Remove all "handicapping apparatus," and read the Scripture. Lead the Share and Commit sections.

Share: What was it like to have the blindfold on or the earplugs in? How did it feel when you removed them? Do you think that the people of Jesus' time who were cured felt the same?

Jesus' time on earth was called "a year of favor from our God." Even though he is not physically with us, he has brought hope and joy. What do you think we could do to remind ourselves that his coming set us free? What do you already do to bring God's year of favor to people today who are blind, handicapped, sick with disease, deaf, dying, or poor? Is it satisfying to you and to them or do you need to consider doing something else?

Commit: This week let's remind ourselves and one another that Jesus wants to give us joy. Let's do something, as individuals or as a family, that shares God's favor with the needy.

Altar Sign: Leave the earplugs and/or the blindfolds on the altar space as a sign of your desire to listen to God and to see with God's vision.

Prayer: God of the lowly and hurting, we thank you for all the ways you have blessed our family. We pray for the grace of joy and hope. We offer ourselves to be a sign of your life in the world. Amen.

Close: Hug one another, and enjoy your treats.

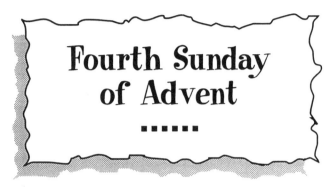

Fourth Sunday of Advent

Theme: God is with us.

Reading: *Matthew 1:18-23 (Gospel)*
This is how the birth of Jesus Christ came about. When his mother Mary was engaged to Joseph, but before they lived together, she was found with child through the power of the Holy Spirit. Joseph, her husband, an upright man unwilling to expose her to the Law, decided to divorce her quietly. Such was his intention when suddenly the angel of the Lord appeared in a dream and said to him: "Joseph, son of David, have no fear about taking Mary as your wife. It is by the Holy Spirit that she has conceived this child. She is to have a son and you are to name him Jesus because he will save his people from their sins." All this happened to fulfill what the Lord had said through the prophet: "The virgin shall be with child and give birth to a son, and they shall call him Emmanuel," a name which means "God is with us."

Materials: ✓ index cards (one per person with his or her name on it) ✓ smaller pieces of paper with the word GOD on each (one per person) ✓ tape ✓ Advent candles (optional)

Treat: caramels or similar chewy, sticky candy, with or without sugar

Leader's Instructions: Gather the family, open with prayer, and read the Scripture. Place the index cards in the middle of the family gathering. Using tape, attach one of the pieces of paper with GOD on it to each person's card. While you're doing this, explain "God is as close to you as the card and paper are to each other. Sometimes, though, we pull away from God." (When you say this, take each card off the GOD sign.) Lead the Share and Commit sections.

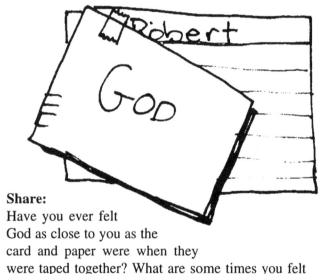

Share:
Have you ever felt God as close to you as the card and paper were when they were taped together? What are some times you felt God that close to you? (Allow persons to share their responses if they like.)

Have you ever felt yourself "pull away" from God? What were the reasons?

How did you "reattach" to God—or do you still feel far away? How can we, as a family, help one another when one of us is not feeling too attached to God?

God is attached to, committed to, and loves each of us individually. What special times does our family celebrate God's attachment and commitment and love for each of us?

Commit: Let's take some quiet time each day this week to feel God's closeness. We might want to go outside, visit a church, or find some other quiet place.

Altar Sign: Lay each person's card, with GOD attached, on the altar space as a sign of God being with you as you uniquely need and accept God.

Prayer: God of the universe, God ever close to us, help us open our hearts to you. We pray for ourselves when we feel distant, and we ask your blessing on all those who think you have left them. May we all live with you forever. Amen.

Close: Hug each person, and say, "This hug is from God." Share the treats.

THE SEASON OF
CHRISTMAS

Holy Family

(SUNDAY IN THE OCTAVE OF CHRISTMAS)

Theme: We put on love.

Reading: *Colossians 3:12-17 (Reading II)*
Because you are God's chosen ones, holy and beloved, clothe yourselves with heartfelt mercy, with kindness, humility, meekness, and patience. Bear with one another; forgive whatever grievances you have against one another. Forgive as the Lord has forgiven you. Over all these virtues put on love, which binds the rest together and makes them perfect. Christ's peace must reign in your hearts, since as members of the one body you have been called to that peace. Dedicate yourselves to thankfulness. Let the word of Christ, rich as it is, dwell in you. In wisdom made perfect, instruct and admonish one another. Sing gratefully to God from your hearts in psalms, hymns, and inspired songs. Whatever you do, whether in speech or in action, do it in the name of the Lord Jesus.

Materials: ✓ piece of material about 12 by 16 inches (or a piece of thin cardboard the same size) ✓ other scraps of material or pieces of construction paper glue ✓ scissors ✓ Christmas candles (optional)

Treat: Fruit Roll-Ups™

Leader's Instructions: Gather the family and place all the materials within the family circle. Open with prayer, and read the Scripture. Ask family members to decide on a symbol for each of the virtues read in the passage.

Cut these symbols out of material scraps or paper. Cut the large piece of material into the shape of a cape. Ask the family to remember times when those virtues have been evident in people's behavior. As these times are named, glue a symbol of that virtue onto the cape. Continue until both sides of the cape are filled or until no one can come up with any other examples of virtues. Lead the Share and Commit sections.

Share:
Notice whether you feel better or worse than you did before the "cape-filling" exercise. Most of us feel better because we've been complimented, and the things we usually take for granted have been noticed.

What virtues were easy for you? Why? Which virtues were harder for you? Why? What do you need to do to increase those virtues?

Commit: Let's agree to compliment one another at least once a day on something they did that pleases us. Let's try to work on the virtue that is especially hard for us to practice.

Altar Sign: Place the cape on the altar space to remind the family to act in ways that are merciful, kind, humble, loving, patient, and forgiving.

Prayer: God of goodness, we thank you for this time together and for the Holy Family that inspires us with their goodness. We ask that you bless our time together and remind us to compliment one another every day. May we continue to love you and one another. Amen.

Close: Share a hug, and say the phrase "...over all your virtues, put on love." Share the treat.

Second Sunday After Christmas

Theme: Jesus is the light of the world.

Reading: *John 1:1-5, 9-14 (Gospel)*
In the beginning was the word; the word was in God's presence, and the word was God. He was present to God in the beginning. Through him all things came into being, and apart from him nothing came to be. Whatever came to be in him, found life, life for the light of people. The light shines on in darkness, a darkness that did not overcome it. The real light that gives light to every person was coming into the world. He was in the world, and through him the world was made, yet the world did not know who he was. To his own he came, yet his own did not accept him. Any who did accept him, he empowered to become children of God. The word became flesh and made his dwelling among us, and we have seen his glory: the glory of an only Son coming from the Father, filled with enduring love.

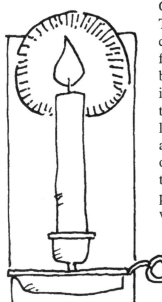

Materials: ✓ one main candle ✓ one candle at each person's place, including the leader. (If there aren't enough candleholders, use a lump of clay in which to anchor a candle in front of each person.)

Treat: candy canes, with or without sugar, as desired

Leader's Instructions: Gather the family, light the main candle, and turn off all other lights in the room. Open with prayer, and read the Scripture by candlelight. When you come to the part "the real light gives light to every person," light each person's individual candle. Continue with the reading, and lead the Share and Commit sections.

Share: Has there ever been a time when you felt scared or overwhelmed by being alone or in the dark? At that time, did you remember Jesus was with you? What helps you remember that Jesus is with you? When you feel scared or anxious, what would you like the family to do to remind you that Jesus is with you? How could you help others in the family with their fear or anxiety?

(Extinguish individual candles, and continue.) Christmas celebrates Jesus dwelling among us, living with us. As a sign of this, each of you may keep your individual candle in a special place. (*CAUTION:* Do not give permission for this if you think it is unwise in your family. Instead, put all the candles on the altar space. Explain to small children that if they want their candle lit, they must have an adult with them and must be supervised while the candle remains lit.)

Commit: This week, let's remember to call on Jesus when we feel lonely, hopeless, or scared.

Altar Sign: Place the main candle on the altar space as a sign of the light of Christ and his enduring love.

Prayer: God of light and goodness, we thank you for Jesus, who shares his light and warmth with us. We pray for the grace to always turn to him in time of darkness or trouble, that we might never lose hope. Amen.

Close: Share a hug with each family member, and pass around the treats.

Materials: ✓ varieties of maps of places your family has been (neighborhood, city, state, or country maps)
✓ blank pieces of paper (one per person)
✓ colored pencils or crayons
✓ Christmas candles
(optional)

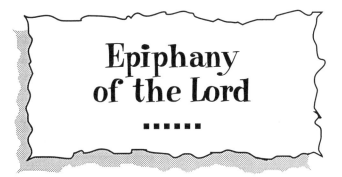

Epiphany of the Lord
■■■■■

Treat: foods that your family packs for a trip (beef jerky, dried fruit)

Leader's Instructions: Gather the family, and open with prayer. Look at the maps, showing the places where your family has been. Remember some of the feelings you had on those trips.

Read the Scripture, pass each person a piece of paper and pencil, and lead the Share and Commit sections.

Theme:
We journey to find the Savior.

Reading: *Matthew 2:1-3, 9-12 (Gospel)*
After Jesus' birth in Bethlehem of Judea during the reign of King Herod, astrologers from the east arrived one day in Jerusalem inquiring, "Where is the new-born king of the Jews? We observed his star at its rising and have come to pay him homage." At this news, King Herod became greatly disturbed, and called the astrologers aside and sent them to Bethlehem.

After their audience with the king, they set out. The star that they had observed at its rising went ahead of them until it came to a standstill over the place where the child was. They were overjoyed at seeing the star, and on entering the house, found the child with Mary, his mother. They prostrated themselves and did him homage. Then they opened their coffers and presented him with gifts of gold, frankincense, and myrrh.

Share: Just as the astrologers went on a journey to find Jesus, we go on a journey to find Jesus too. Our journeys might not take us out of this town, but we still have events that are special times on our journeys. Today, each of us will make a time line of our journey with Christ, starting with your birth. Put on your time line any event that made you feel close to God and any event that made you feel far from God, using different colored pencils or crayons. Include the special people who showed God's love to you. (Younger children will need help in making their time line.)

Birth

Our journeys are not over. Each day we have the chance to walk closer to God. Think about times coming up that might be "forks" in the road, when you will have a chance to choose God or take another path. What helps you stay on the "right path"?

Commit: This week, let's pay special attention to those times when we feel close to God and the times we feel we have a decision to choose God or another path. Let's do whatever it is that helps us stay on the right path.

Altar Sign: Place the time lines on the altar space as a reminder of your journeys in Christ, traveled step by step, each moment and decision of each day.

Prayer: God, our creator and guide, watch over us and keep us faithful to you. May we grow to know you, love you, and serve you more every day. Amen.

Close: Give one another a hug with the words, "Have a good journey," and share the treat.

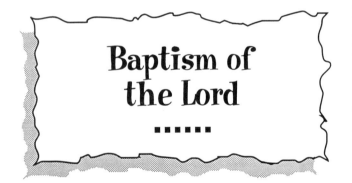

Baptism of the Lord

■■■■■■

Theme: You are God's beloved.

Reading: *Matthew 3:13-17 (Gospel)*
Jesus, coming from Galilee, appeared before John at the Jordan to be baptized by him. John tried to refuse him with the protest, "I should be baptized by you, yet you come to me!" Jesus answered, "Give in for now. We must do this if we would fulfill all of God's demands." So John gave in.

After Jesus was baptized, he came directly out of the water. Suddenly the sky opened, and he saw the Spirit of God descend like a dove and hover over him. With that, a voice from the heavens said, "This is my beloved Son. My favor rests on him."

Materials: ✓ an artificial white bird or one made from paper (See Appendix B on page 91.) ✓ Christmas candles (optional)

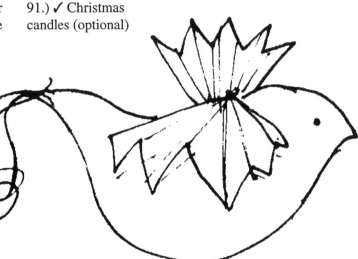

Treat: heart-shaped valentine candy, with or without sugar

Leader's Instructions: Gather the family and put the white bird in the middle of the gathering. Open with prayer, read the Scripture, and lead the Share and Commit sections.

Share: Last week we talked about times we have felt close to God. Does anyone have anything they would like to share about how their week went? (Allow time for everyone to share if they like.)

This week we see God revealing love for Jesus. What do you think it might have been like when that happened? If you were Jesus then, how do you think you would have felt? Imagine that God also wants to say the same thing to us. How does it feel? scary? good?

Because of our baptism in Christ, we have also become God's beloved sons and daughters. We will each take a turn holding the dove, while the rest of us reminds that person of that baptismal truth: "You are precious to God." (Give one person the dove to hold. While that person holds the dove, direct the rest of the family members to say, "_____[person's name]_____, you are God's beloved son/daughter." Continue moving the dove around until all members have had a turn.)

Commit: During this week, let's remember that we are beloved of God, just as we are. Let's each think of a place, a prayer, a thing, or a person that reminds us of God's love for us. Let's use that place, prayer, thing, or person to help us remember God's love.

Altar Sign: Place the bird on the altar space to remind the family that the Spirit of God hovers over and around each of them with love.

Prayer: God, our father, we thank you for including us in your family. We pray to be worthy to be called your sons and daughters. We ask for the grace to live each day as your child. Amen.

Close: Share a hug, and enjoy the treat.

THE SEASON OF
ORDINARY
TIME

Second Sunday in Ordinary Time

■■■■■■

Theme: We recognize God.

Reading: *John 1:29, 31-34 (Gospel)*
When John caught sight of Jesus coming toward him, he exclaimed: "Look there! The Lamb of God who takes away the sin of the world! I confess I did not recognize him, though the very reason I came baptizing with water was that he might be revealed to Israel."

John gave this testimony also: "I saw the Spirit descend like a dove from the sky, and it came to rest on him. But, as I say, I did not recognize him. The One who sent me to baptize with water told me, 'When you see the Spirit descend and rest on someone, it is he who is to baptize with the Holy Spirit.' Now I have seen for myself and have testified, 'This is God's Chosen One.'"

Materials: ✓ various pictures of Jesus (Sacred Heart, Good Shepherd, Jesus watching over the world, a popular painting, the image from the Shroud, and so forth) ✓ blank paper ✓ crayons, markers, or colored pencils

Treat: Tootsie Roll Pops™ or a similar "surprise-inside" candy

Leader's Instructions: Gather the family and open with prayer. Set out whatever pictures of Jesus you have gathered. Read the Scripture, and lead the Share and Commit sections.

Share: These pictures are familiar to us; we would probably know who it is in the picture because of the Bible stories we have heard or because we have seen something like them before. John the Baptist was at a disadvantage because he did not know who the Chosen One was.

Which of the pictures do you like best? Why? Does the picture remind you of how it felt last week when you remembered you were loved by God? How *did* it feel when you remembered that?

Using the paper and whatever writing utensils you like, draw a symbol of how God's presence or love felt.

Might there be times that God is with *us*, calling us to do something? How do we hear this "call"? What about those times when we don't want to recognize that God is calling us? What should we do then? How can we help one another listen to God and/or recognize the call?

Commit: This week, let's pay attention to those times we think God might be "calling" us. Let's ask one another to help us recognize whether or not God actually is calling.

Altar Sign: Place the pictures and symbols on the altar space as a sign of the many unique ways you experience God's presence.

Prayer: God, our creator, you know us through and through. We pray for the grace to listen to you with our hearts and minds and wills. May we always grow in unity with you and Christ and the Holy Spirit. Amen.

Close: Share a hug, and enjoy your treat.

Third Sunday in Ordinary Time

∎∎∎∎∎∎

Theme: We follow Jesus.

Reading: *Matthew 4:12-13, 17-22 (Gospel)*
When Jesus heard that John had been arrested, he withdrew to Galilee. He left Nazareth and went down to live in Capernaum. From that time on, Jesus began to proclaim this theme: "Reform your lives! The reign of God is at hand."

As he was walking along the Sea of Galilee, he watched two brothers—Simon now known as Peter, and his brother Andrew—casting a net into the sea. They were fishermen. He said to them, "Come after me and I will make you fishers of men and women and children." They immediately abandoned their nets and became his followers.

He walked along farther and caught sight of two other brothers, James, Zebedee's son, and his brother John. They, too, were in their boat, getting their nets in order with their father. Jesus called them and immediately they abandoned the boat and their father to follow him.

Jesus toured all of Galilee. He taught in the synagogues, proclaimed the good news of the reign of God, and cured the people of every disease and illness.

Materials:
✓ fish bowl ✓ fishing pole ✓ fish net (or fish hook used with caution) ✓ slips of paper (one per person) ✓ one piece of blank paper on which you traced the outline of a sandal

Treat: fish crackers or fruit leather

Leader's Instructions: Gather the family, and place in the center of the group whatever fishing equipment you have chosen. Read the Scripture, and lead the Share and Commit sections.

Share: Sometimes it is hard to believe that people would just drop everything and follow Jesus. They must have been unsatisfied with their lives and saw in him the key to a special purpose and meaning in their lives.

Is there anything about your life that you are dissatisfied with? Are you open to Jesus leading you in this area, in search of satisfaction? If Jesus were to ask you today to reform your life and follow him, what is it that you would need to reform, or what might you leave behind? (At this point, have each person write on a slip of paper what he or she would need to leave behind. Put these slips of paper into the fish bowl or net, or attach them to the fish hook.)

If we leave these things behind, what is it that we should do instead to "fish" for people, bringing them to God? What should we do instead to follow Jesus? (Ask someone to write these responses on the sandal as a sign of following Jesus.) Will it be hard to do these things? How can we encourage one another to make it easier?

Commit: This week, let's leave behind everything we feel Jesus is asking us to leave. Let's follow Jesus in the particular way we have written on the sandal.

Altar Sign: Place the fishing item and the paper sandal on the altar space as an encouragement to follow Jesus in the ways the family just discussed.

Prayer: Dear God, you are constantly calling us further from things that "hook" us and closer to following your Son, Jesus. We pray for the grace to carry out our commitments this week, that we might truly be fishers of all people for you. Amen.

Close: Share a hug, try on one another's shoes, and enjoy your treat.

Fourth Sunday in Ordinary Time

......

Theme: Beatitudes are a paradox.

Reading: *Matthew 5:1-12 (Gospel)*
When Jesus saw the crowds, he went up on the mountainside. After his disciples sat down around him, he began to teach them: "How blest are the poor in spirit: the reign of God is theirs. Blest, too, are the sorrowing; they shall be consoled. Blest are the lowly; they shall inherit the land. Blest are they who hunger and thirst for holiness; they shall have their fill. Blest are they who show mercy; mercy shall be theirs. Blest are the single-hearted, for they shall see God. Blest, too, are the peacemakers; they shall be called sons and daughters of God. Blest are those persecuted for holiness' sake; the reign of God is theirs. Blest are you when they insult you and persecute you and utter every kind of slander against you because of me. Be glad and rejoice, for your reward in heaven is great."

Materials: ✓ tracing of a face-vase picture (See Appendix C on page 92.)

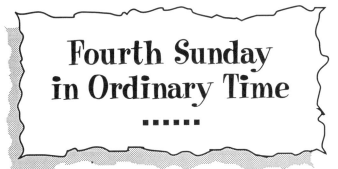

Treat: yogurt-covered pretzels

Leader's Instructions: Prepare the face-vase picture ahead of time. Gather the family, and open with prayer. Read the Scripture, and display the face-vase. Draw the family's attention to the fact that depending on how you look at the face-vase picture, you see one of two things: a vase or the silhouette of two faces looking at each other. Lead the Share and Commit sections.

Share: Just like this picture is confusing, so are the beatitudes, because it's hard to understand why people should be told that they are happy or blest in a bad situation.

Has there been a time when you were feeling blest in spite of a bad situation? What happened? Were you surprised at your feelings? Which of the beatitudes can you identify with most at this time? (Ask someone to write the reasons on the "face.") Which one might you be a little afraid of at this time of your life? (Ask someone to write the responses on the "vase.")

Depending on your situation, you might be able to handle these situations later in life. Something that seems very confusing now might not be confusing later.

Commit: This week, let's trust in God no matter what the situation is.

Altar Sign: Place the vase-face picture with the family responses on it on the altar space to remind everyone to trust God no matter what the situation.

Prayer: Dear God, you call us to a have an attitude about life that is different from the attitude of the world. We pray for the grace to always trust you no matter what the situation. Amen.

Close: Share a hug, and enjoy the treat.

Fifth Sunday in Ordinary Time

▪▪▪▪▪▪

Theme: We are the salt of the earth.

Reading: *Matthew 5:13-16 (Gospel)*
Jesus said to his disciples: "You are the salt of the earth. But what if salt goes flat? How can you restore its flavor? Then it is good for nothing but to be thrown out and trampled underfoot. You are the light of the world. A city set on a hill cannot be hidden. People do not light a lamp and then put it under a bushelbasket. They set it on a stand where it gives light to all in the house. In the same way, your light must shine before all people so that they may see goodness in your acts and give praise to God in heaven."

Materials: ✓ light bulb (use caution around small children)

Treat: crackers with salt and crackers without salt, or biscuits made from scratch—some with salt, some without

Leader's Instructions: Gather the family, and place the light bulb in the center of the group. Read the Scripture, and lead the Share and Commit sections.

Share: How are people like a light bulb? Could a person shine on his or her own?

(Pass around the unsalted treat, and ask everyone to take a taste.) Notice how plain these crackers/biscuits are; they lack salt. Just as salt makes a difference in the taste of these crackers/biscuits, courage makes a difference in a person's life. But how? What qualities besides courage would you find in a person who is "salt" for God? Do you think there are any ways that the "salt" (those "special" qualities) can be restored in a person?

Has there been a time when you have been "salt" or "light" for God? Is there a situation in which you find it hard to be "salt" or "light" for God? How could our family help you in this kind of situation?

Commit:
This week, let's be "salt" or "light" for God, especially in a situation that has been hard for us.

Altar Sign: Place the light bulb on the altar space. (If there are young children around who might pull it off and be hurt, put it up high or secure it in a see-through food container.) You could also use a salt shaker or a box of salt. The salt or light will serve as a reminder to be courageous in bringing God's goodness to the world.

Prayer: God of salt and light, we thank you for the way you restore our faith in you. We pray for the grace to bring goodness to the world this week. Amen.

Close: Share a hug, and share the rest of the treat.

Sixth Sunday in Ordinary Time

■ ■ ■ ■ ■ ■

Theme: God's commands bring forth our goodness.

Reading: *Matthew 5:20-22, 27-28, 33-34, 37 (Gospel)*
Jesus said to his disciples: "I tell you, unless your holiness surpasses that of the scribes and Pharisees you shall not enter the reign of God. You have heard the commandment imposed on your ancestors, 'You shall not commit murder; every murderer will be liable to judgment.' What I say to you is: everyone who grows angry with a brother or a sister will be liable to judgment. You have heard the commandment, 'You shall not commit adultery.' What I say to you is: anyone who looks lustfully at another has already committed adultery in his or her thoughts. You have heard the commandment imposed on your ancestors, 'Do not take a false oath; rather, make good to God all your pledges.' What I tell you is: do not swear at all. Say 'Yes' when you mean 'Yes' and 'No' when you mean 'No.'"

Materials: ✓ one opened-out-flat facial tissue for each person (or pieces of white tissue paper or pieces of multicolored tissue paper cut to facial-tissue size) ✓ one six-inch length of string or one rubber band for each person

Treat: sliced apples or oranges, wedged into six or eight sections that are not cut all the way through so the sections can be spread out like a flower

Leader's Instructions: Gather the family, and open with prayer. Read the Scripture, and lead the Share and Commit sections.

Share: Jesus came and tightened the rules so that we could be as pure of heart as possible. He knew that purity of heart was necessary for holiness. So we need to try as best as we can to do what he says.

(Give each person a piece of tissue.) Fold this piece of tissue like an accordion, in pleats about one-half inch wide. (Younger children may need help. Continue the discussion while the tissue is being folded.) Are there times when God's commands or rules feel tight or "cramp your style"? If this was in the past, and you followed the rule, have you seen how you were better off?

Jesus' new rules were intended to lead us toward respect for others and toward holiness. Would this happen if we listened to him? What are the situations in which we usually get angry? greedy? are tempted to lie? Can these situations be avoided? How could family members help one another through the temptations?

(When each person finishes folding his or her tissue, tie a string tightly around the middle. Carefully pull each layer of tissue toward the center, forming a puffy flower.)

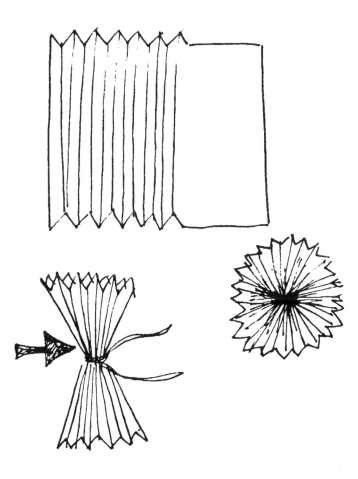

Commit: This week, let's each change one behavior and ask for help from the family as we do this.

Altar Sign: Place the puffy flowers on the altar space as a sign of the beauty that will shine forth if you truly follow the commands of God.

Prayer: Dear God, you sent Jesus to earth to be one of us and to lead us to you. We pray for the grace to listen to his words and make them come alive in our lives. Amen.

Close: Share a hug, and enjoy the treat.

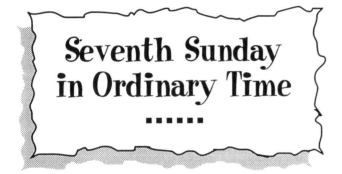

Seventh Sunday in Ordinary Time

Theme: God's way will open our hearts.

Reading: *Matthew 5:38-48 (Gospel)*
Jesus said to his disciples: "You have heard the commandment, 'An eye for an eye, a tooth for a tooth.' But what I say to you is: offer no resistance to injury. When a person strikes you on the right cheek, turn and offer the other. If anyone wants to go to the law over your shirt, hand over your coat as well. Should anyone press you into service for one mile, go with that person two miles. Give to the one who begs from you. Do not turn your back on the borrower. You have heard the commandment, 'You shall love those of your country but hate your enemy.' My command to you is: love your enemies, pray for your persecutors. This will prove that you are children of God in heaven, whose sun rises on the bad and the good and who rains on the just and the unjust. If you love those who love you, what merit is there in that. Do not the tax collectors do as much? And if you greet your brothers and sisters only, what is so praiseworthy in that? Do not the pagans do as much? In a word, you must be perfected, as God in heaven is perfect."

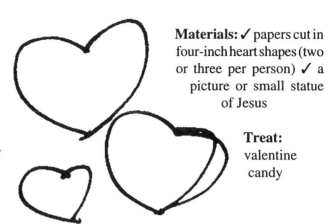

Materials: ✓ papers cut in four-inch heart shapes (two or three per person) ✓ a picture or small statue of Jesus

Treat: valentine candy

Leader's Instructions: Gather the family, open with prayer, and place the heart papers in the center of the group. Explain that during the past week valentines expressing love and care were sent and received. Go on to explain that this week Jesus asks us to consider sending valentines to our enemies and persecutors, people who have hurt us. After explaining this, read the Scripture, and lead the Share and Commit sections.

Share: We won't really have to send more valentines, but on the heart-shaped papers, write the first name or the initials of someone whom you have a grudge against or who persecuted you or whom you consider your enemy. Think for a minute now about what happened to cause your feelings against this person. Can you think of how it *hurts you* to hang onto these hurt feelings? What is being accomplished by your hurt and anger? Is there a way to accomplish that by some other means? Can you believe that these persons are sons and daughters of God, loved by God, even though their actions might not have been of God? Can you at least wish them goodness? For our own sakes, we need to rid ourselves of vengeance.

Bow your head, close your eyes, imagine that Jesus is next to you, even has his arm around you. Think about the persons you have hard feelings toward. In your imagination, tell them that you wish them peace. Let the strength and love of Jesus come into you as he holds you. Tell the persons, in your imagination, that you forgive them. (Listen to the quiet for a few moments.)

Commit: This week, let's pray for the grace to forgive those persons whenever hardness of heart against them tries to sneak back into our hearts.

Altar Sign: Place the initialed papers on the altar space, with the picture or statue of Jesus next to them, as signs of the power of forgiveness through the love of Christ.

Prayer: Dear God, you know our hearts and our desire to be close to you. We pray for the grace to turn to you instead of fostering hatred and meanness in our hearts. We pray for the grace to be at peace. Amen.

Close: Share a hug, and enjoy the treat.

Eighth Sunday in Ordinary Time
■■■■■■

Theme: We will not worry.

Reading: *Matthew 6:24-34 (Gospel)*
Jesus said to his disciples: "No one can serve two masters. You will either hate one and love the other, or be attentive to one and despise the other. You cannot give yourself to God and money. I warn you, then; do not worry about your livelihood, what you are to eat or drink or use for clothing. Is not life more than food? Is not the body more valuable than clothes? Look at the birds in the sky. They do not sow or reap, they gather nothing into barns; yet your God in heaven feeds them. Are you not more important than they? Which of you by worrying can add a moment to your life span? Learn a lesson from the way the wildflowers grow. They do not work; they do not spin. Yet I assure you, not even Solomon in all his splendor was arrayed like one of these. If God can clothe in such splendor the grass of the field which blooms today and is thrown on the fire tomorrow, will God not provide much more for you, O weak in faith! Stop worrying, then, over questions like 'What are we to eat or what are we to drink or what are we to wear?' The believers are always running after these things. Your heavenly God knows all that you need. Seek first God's reign over you, God's way of holiness, and all these things will be given you besides. Do not worry about tomorrow; tomorrow will take care of itself."

Materials: ✓ fresh flowers (one per person) ✓ one vase ✓ one index card ✓ one pencil

Treat: grapes (none sour!)

Leader's Instructions: Gather the family, and offer a flower to each person, letting him or her hold it as you open with prayer, read the Scripture, and lead the Share and Commit sections.

Share: Worrying means we have given something else first place in our hearts and minds instead of God. We need to free ourselves of all worries.

What things do you always worry about—even small things? Does worrying help? How or why not? Is there a way to accomplish any positive side effects without worrying? What things do you miss in the present moment when you worry? Have you ever looked back and regretted the time you spent worrying? Have you tried to stop worrying? How? How can family members help you stop worrying? What can you tell yourself to remind you to live in the "now" and not worry? (Ask someone to write responses on the index card.)

Commit: This week, let's remind ourselves of whatever we wrote on the card. Let's try to help one another to stop worrying.

Altar Sign: Place all the flowers in the vase. Set the vase on the altar, and set the index card against the vase as a reminder of what each will use to "turn off" the worry.

Prayer: O God, creator of the flowers and birds and us, we want to believe that you are constantly watching out for us, that your love and grace are enough for us. We pray for the grace to stop worrying and, instead, to enjoy every moment of our lives. Amen.

Close: Share a hug, and enjoy the treat.

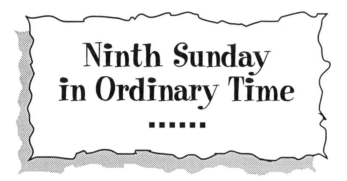

Ninth Sunday in Ordinary Time

Theme: The wise build a firm foundation on Jesus.

Reading: *Matthew 7:24-27 (Gospel)*
Jesus said to his disciples, "Those who hear my words and put them into practice are like the wise who built their houses on rock. When the rainy season set in, the torrents came and the winds blew and buffeted their houses, but they did not collapse; they had been solidly set on rock. Those who hear my words but do not put them into practice are like the foolish ones who built their houses on sandy ground. The rains fell, the torrents came, the winds blew and lashed against their houses, which collapsed under all this, and were completely ruined."

Materials: ✓ ten 3- by 5-inch index cards (or construction paper cut to that size) ✓ one 4- by 6-inch index card (or light-colored piece of construction paper cut to that size) ✓ one can of modeling clay ✓ two cups of sand, cornmeal, or rice ✓ one cookie sheet ✓ pencils ✓ scissors

Treat: rock candy or sugar-free hard candy

Leader's Instructions: Gather the family, and open with prayer. Set the cookie sheet in the middle of the family group, placing on it the modeling clay and five index cards ("rock cards") at one end and the cups of sand and five index cards ("sand cards") at the other. Read the Scripture, and lead the Share and Commit sections.

Share: We each build a spiritual house by the things we do every day. Building on sand might mean doing things the way everybody else does. Building on sand is taking the easy way out of trouble. Building on a firm foundation might mean apologizing to others, keeping promises, or being nice to persons in our family when you really don't feel like it.

What are some ways we use sand in our spiritual foundation? (Have someone write these ideas on the five "sand cards.") What are some ways we use rock in our spiritual foundation? (Have someone write these ideas on the five "rock cards.")

(As a family, build two "card houses," one with the sand and cards and one with the clay and cards.) It's easy to see which of these houses is going to be a little more solid and sturdy.

What might be some of the "winds" and "rains" we could expect, either in our relationships with one another, between our family and the community, or between ourselves and God? What "storms" have we already gone through? How do you think we did? What helped us? What could we have done better? How, do you think, did God help us? How will we know if God is helping us in the future?

(Cut the two top corners off the big index card so it looks like a house.)

What would each of us be willing to do this week that will build a firm foundation for our own spiritual house? (Ask someone to write these on the house-shaped index card next to each person's name.)

Commit: This week, let's carry out the promises we've each made to build a firm foundation.

Altar Sign: Place the big index card in the clay and set that on the altar space to remind the family of the importance of a firm spiritual foundation.

Prayer: O God, our creator, who made the wind and the rain, the sand, and the rock, we thank you for being with us and for calling us to listen to your words. We pray for the grace to be faithful to our promises this week, and to know you, love you, and serve you always. Amen.

Close: Share a hug, and enjoy the treat.

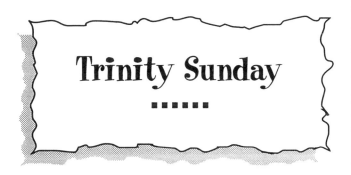

Trinity Sunday

Theme: Gaining eternal life: magic or not?

Reading: *John 3:16-18 (Gospel)*
Jesus said to Nicodemus: "Yes, God so loved the world that he gave his only Son, that whoever believes in him may not die but have eternal life. God did not send the Son into the world to condemn the world, but that the world might be saved through the Son. Whoever believes in the Son avoids condemnation, but whoever does not believe is already condemned for not believing in the name of God's only Son."

Materials: ✓ one thick sheet of paper measuring 6 by 5 inches ✓ ruler ✓ pencil ✓ utility knife or scissors

Treat: M & M's™ or a sugar-free variety

Leader's Instructions: Before you begin this prayer session, become familiar with the directions in Appendix D on page 93 for "paper-folding magic" or be prepared to do a magic trick you already know.

Gather the family, and open with prayer. Show the folded sculpture to those gathered and explain to them that the sculpture is, indeed, one piece of paper. Read the Scripture, and lead the Share and Commit sections.

Share: What is magic? (Listen carefully to everyone's responses.) Magic is usually something we see but don't understand—yet we're sure we could learn the techniques and do the magic ourselves.

What about eternal life? Does Scripture say we get eternal life just like magic, just by saying, "Oh, I believe"? (No.) No, because to believe in something, we must learn about it.

Believing in Jesus means we keep learning what Jesus stands for, why he was given to us, and what power we have through him. Believing means we have even "tried" him for ourselves, and we want to be with him forever. When we do this, we feel "saved." Those who don't believe often feel pretty hopeless inside.

What are some of the things you believe about Jesus? How did you come to believe these things? How would your outlook on life be different if you did not believe in Jesus?

How about the way you treat others and interact with them? How about your goals in life? How about the ways you handle hard times? How are all of these different because you believe in Jesus?

Are you glad you believe in Jesus? How might you share your belief in Jesus with others? How could the family share in your belief of Jesus? How can our family support your belief in Jesus?

Commit: At least once this week, let's share our belief in Jesus with someone.

Altar Sign: Place the magic-trick materials on the altar space as a sign of your need to understand, to learn about, and to "try" Jesus for yourselves.

Prayer: Dear God, we thank you for your love that reaches out to us in Jesus. We pray for the grace to know his presence in our lives every day, that we might be strengthened in our belief in him and so live with you and him and the Holy Spirit forever. Amen.

Close: Share a hug, and invite others to do magic tricks they know. Enjoy the treat.

Body and Blood of Christ

■ ■ ■ ■ ■

Theme: "Those who eat this bread shall live forever."

Reading: *John 6:51-58 (Gospel)*
Jesus said to the crowds of Jews, "I myself am the living bread come down from heaven. If anyone eats this bread, that one shall live forever; the bread I will give is my flesh, for the life of the world."

At this the Jews quarreled among themselves, saying, "How can he give us his flesh to eat?" Thereupon Jesus said to them, "Let me solemnly assure you, if you do not eat the flesh of the Son of Man and drink his blood, you have no life in you. The one who feeds on my flesh and drinks my blood has life eternal, and I will raise that one up on the last day. For my flesh is real food and my blood is real drink. You who feed on my flesh and drink my blood remain in me and I in you. Just as God who has life sent me, and I have life because of God, so you who feed on me will have life because of me. This is the bread that came down from heaven. Unlike your ancestors who ate and died nonetheless, you who feed on this bread shall live forever."

Materials: ✓ Mass booklet (or Sunday missal that includes the parts of the Mass) ✓ a piece of paper or poster with a line drawn down the middle to indicate two columns; mark one column INPUT and the other OUTPUT

Treat: pita bread or homemade loaf of bread

Leader's Instructions: Gather the family, and lead opening prayer. Remind the family of the discussion about magic from last week. Explain that this week has a similar potential for being seen as "magic" especially the part in Scripture about "eat this and live forever." Read the Scripture, and lead the Share and Commit sections.

Share: (Hold up the paper or poster.) Going to Mass and receiving Communion is not magic. What we receive from attending Mass and receiving Communion depends on what we put into it. If we just put in our time at Mass, what are we likely to get? (Ask someone to write the responses in the column marked INPUT.) If we open ourselves to God, what are we likely to get? (Ask someone to write the responses in the column marked OUTPUT.)

How could a person "open" himself or herself to God at Mass? What might you say to a person who says the church would tumble to the ground if he or she stepped into it? What might you say to a person who attends Mass but doesn't feel worthy of receiving Communion?

What experiences have you had of receiving the body and blood of Christ and having it be a life-giving experience? What makes you more open to God at Mass? What detracts from your experience of God at Mass? What kind of preparation helps you be more open to God? How could the family support you in preparing to be more open to God at Mass?

Commit: This week, let's prepare ourselves to be more open to God at Mass. Let's help one another in this preparation.

Altar Sign: Hang the INPUT/OUTPUT poster on the wall by the altar space as a reminder of your need to prepare yourselves for Mass. The Mass booklet or missal can be placed on the altar space as well for those who want to use it to help with that preparation.

Prayer: Dear Jesus, you willingly sacrificed yourself to be life for us. We thank you. We pray for the grace to treasure Mass and Communion, that we each might be transformed into the people you desire. Amen.

Close: Offer hugs all around, and enjoy the treat.

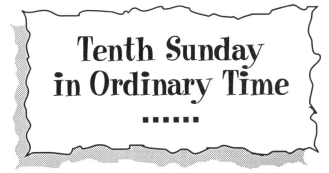

Tenth Sunday in Ordinary Time

∎∎∎∎∎

Theme: It is mercy God desires, not just sacrifice.

Reading: *Matthew 9:9-13 (Gospel)*
As Jesus moved about, he saw a man named Matthew at his post where taxes were collected. Jesus said to him, "Follow me." Matthew got up and followed him.

Now it happened that, while Jesus was at table in Matthew's home, many tax collectors and those known as sinners came to join him and his disciples at dinner. The Pharisees saw this and complained to his disciples, "What reason can the Teacher have for eating with tax collectors and those who disregard the law?" Overhearing the remark, Jesus said, "People who are in good health do not need a doctor; sick people do. Go and learn the meaning of the words, 'It is mercy I desire and not sacrifice.' I have come to call not the self-righteous, but the sinners."

Materials: ✓ birthday hats ✓ one sheet of notebook paper per person ✓ balloons

Treat: birthday cake

Leader's Instructions: Blow up some balloons beforehand and have the cake made and decorated. You might decorate the cake with the words "Happy mercy to us." Familiarize yourself with how to make the paper blowers (Appendix E on page 94). You will teach the family how to make the blowers when you share the treat. Gather the family, open with prayer, and read the Scripture. Lead the Share and Commit sections.

Share: The word for *mercy* in Hebrew comes from the word *hessed*. The word means "undeserved kindness." In remembrance of God's undeserved kindness to us, we give ourselves a birthday party, since our very lives were not earned but are God's gift to us.

Has anyone ever been kind to you when you felt like you didn't deserve it? How did you feel? What did you want to do? Have you ever felt that kindness from God? Have you ever felt like you've gotten a second chance at life or a job or a relationship?

Have there been times when you didn't think God was merciful at all? Do you still feel that way? If so, how can the family help you in this or support you in healing? If you no longer feel that way, what happened to help you view God differently?

Do you think all followers of Christ are considered sinners? Where would you place yourself on a "self-righteous-sinner" continuum?

When Jesus says that God wants mercy, not sacrifice, does he mean that we should never make sacrifices? How might mercy involve sacrifice?

Commit: Each day this week, let's do an act of mercy, especially for one another.

Altar Sign: After the family shares the treat, place the party hats and blowers on the altar space to remind the family of the many reasons they have to be grateful to God. (If you feel especially grateful one day, why not put on a hat or take a turn with the blower and let your family celebrate with you.)

Prayer: O good God, we thank you for our lives. We pray for the grace to see your mercy in our everyday lives. We pray for the grace to treat others with this same undeserved kindness. Amen.

Close: Make the paper blowers, share a family hug, cut the cake, and enjoy!

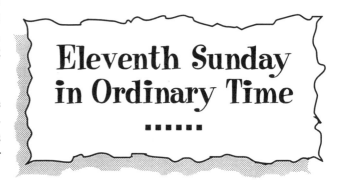

Eleventh Sunday in Ordinary Time
■■■■■

Theme: God needs laborers for "the harvest."

Reading: *Matthew 9:36–10:1, 5-8 (Gospel)*
At the sight of the crowds, the heart of Jesus was moved with pity. They were lying prostrate from exhaustion, like sheep without a shepherd. Jesus said to his disciples: "The harvest is good but laborers are scarce. Beg the harvest master to send out laborers to gather the harvest." Then he summoned the Twelve and gave them authority to expel unclean spirits and cure sickness and disease of every kind. Jesus sent these on mission after giving them the following instructions: "Do not visit pagan territory and do not enter a Samaritan town. Go instead after the lost sheep of the house of Israel. As you go, make this announcement: 'The reign of God is at hand!' Cure the sick, raise the dead, heal the lepers, expel demons. The gift you have received, give as a gift."

Materials: ✓ a basket (any size) ✓ three slips of paper (different colors) ✓ one pencil

Treat: cantaloupe, watermelon, or other fruit

Leader's Instructions: Gather the family, and open with prayer. Explain to those gathered that last week the family committed to acts of mercy as a response to God's constant mercy. This week, we are asked to respond so intensely as to be called "laborers." Read the Scripture, and lead the Share and Commit sections.

Share: How does it feel to hear that God needs you as a laborer? In what ways are you already laboring for God? (Ask someone to write the responses on one sheet of colored paper.) Do you find it satisfying and renewing to do these labors, or are they more trouble than they're worth? If they're more trouble than they're worth, would you consider not doing them?

The Twelve were sent to those situations and people whom they knew well. Who are some of the people (by name or by group) whose experiences you can identify with? (Ask someone to write the responses on another sheet of colored paper.) How might God need you to labor with them? Could your family support you in this—or might it be a family labor? (Ask someone to write the responses on the third sheet of colored paper.)

Commit: This week, let's decide on a way to labor for God in a new way, as individuals or as a family.

Altar Sign: Place the three colored sheets of paper in the basket, and place the basket on the altar space as a reminder to be open to how God might need you this week.

Prayer: Dear God, who sees all that can be and needs to be, we thank you for the gifts you have given us as family. We pray that we may be open to hearing your word to us. We pray for the grace to do your will as laborers of the harvest. Amen.

Close: Share a hug, and enjoy your treat.

Twelfth Sunday in Ordinary Time
■■■■■■

Theme: God knows what is happening in our lives.

Reading: *Matthew 10:26-33 (Gospel)*
Jesus said to his apostles, "Do not let people intimidate you. Nothing is concealed that will not be revealed and nothing hidden that will not become known. What I tell you in darkness, speak in the light. What you hear in private, proclaim from the housetops. Do not fear those who deprive the body of life but cannot destroy the soul. Rather, fear the one who can destroy both body and soul in Gehenna. Are not two sparrows sold for next to nothing? Yet not a single sparrow falls to the ground without the consent of God in heaven. As for you, every hair of your head has been counted; so do not be afraid of anything. You are worth more than an entire flock of sparrows. Whoever acknowledges me before others, I will acknowledge before God in heaven. And whoever disowns me before others, I will disown before God in heaven."

Materials: ✓ personal combs or brushes

Treat: Gummi Bears™ or gum

Leader's Instructions: As you gather the family, ask them to bring their combs or brushes. Say an opening prayer, and ask everyone to place the combs or brushes in the center of the group. Read the Scripture, and lead the Share and Commit sections.

Share: God knows so much about what is happening in our lives that every hair on our head has been counted. How does that feel?

What fears do you have? What kind of person intimidates you? Does Jesus promise we won't get hurt? If we have been hurt, how could we "give away" our soul instead of turning to God?

If you have to deal with intimidating people regularly, what do you think God would like you to do so you would no longer be afraid? Would God object to an "assertiveness" class or a "self-help" book on how to deal with your fear? How do you act when you get anxious or afraid? How could the family help you during these times?

Commit: Every time we brush or comb our hair this week, let's remember God's loving presence, so much love that God knows exactly how many hairs we have on our head.

Altar Sign: Place the comb or brush you brought on the altar space to remind the family that God is aware of all that happens.

Prayer: Heavenly God, sometimes you seem far from us, but today we are reminded that you are very caring and close. We pray for the grace to walk and live in courage this week. We trust you will show us the way in difficult times. Amen.

Close: Give a hug and a pat on the head to one another. Enjoy your treat.

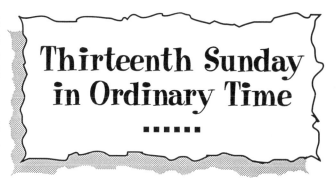

Thirteenth Sunday in Ordinary Time

Theme: We take up our cross and follow Jesus.

Reading: *Matthew 10:37-39 (Gospel)*
Jesus said to his apostles: "Whoever loves father or mother, son or daughter, more than me is not worthy of me. Those who will not take up their cross and come after me are not worthy of me. Those who seek only themselves will bring themselves to ruin, whereas those who bring themselves to nought for me, discover who they are."

Materials: ✓ an upright cross or crucifix (If the crucifix won't stand on its own, place the base of it in a mound of clay.) ✓ crosses cut out of paper (one per person) ✓ tape ✓ pencils (one per person)

Treat: energy bar or granola bar

Leader's Instructions: Gather the family, and open with prayer. Place the standing cross and paper crosses in the middle of the group. Read the Scripture, and lead the Share and Commit sections.

Share: Today, we focus on our crosses. Consider that a cross might be something about yourself that you are stuck with temporarily or permanently (compulsions, memories, health problems). Or your cross might be something about your situation in life that you feel stuck with (job, school, neighbors, brothers, or sisters).

Have you ever had a cross that is, today, no longer a cross? What happened? How did you turn to Jesus in that time?

What things about yourself and/or your life situation are crosses to you today? It doesn't matter if other people don't seem to have a problem with the same situation or person. If it's something you wish you could get rid of, it is a cross to you. Write two or three of your own personal crosses on one of the paper crosses. What is your usual way of dealing with these things? (Ask someone to help younger children with this.)

Jesus recommends picking up the cross. That means we admit something is a cross, we admit we don't like the cross, but we claim it just the same. Many people find that once they realize what their crosses are and admit to them, the crosses are not so heavy. Once they admit to the crosses, they can use the energy they spent fighting the crosses to learn how to cope with them.

What might we do about our crosses if we stopped fighting them? How could we support one another in this? (Ask someone to tape the paper crosses to Jesus' cross as a sign of following him in these areas.)

Commit: This week, let's think about our crosses and try to accept them rather than fight against them.

Altar Sign: Stand the cross with attached paper crosses on the altar space to remind persons that when they pick up their crosses in the Spirit of Christ, the burden will not be so heavy.

Prayer: Dear Jesus, you did not like your cross, but you carried it out of love for us. We pray for wisdom as we carry these crosses out of love for you. We ask your guidance in learning how to cope with them and trust in your goodness and love for us. Amen.

Close: Share a hug with each family member, and eat your treats.

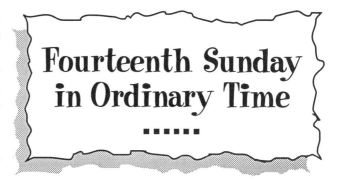

Fourteenth Sunday in Ordinary Time

Theme: Jesus knows the secret of being at peace.

Reading: *Matthew 11:25-30 (Gospel)*
On one occasion Jesus spoke thus: "Father, God of heaven and earth, to you I offer praise; for what you have hidden from the learned and the clever you have revealed to the merest children. It is true. you have graciously willed it so. Everything has been given over to me by you. Come to me, all you who are weary and find life burdensome, and I will refresh you. Take my yoke upon your shoulders and learn from me, for I am gentle and humble of heart. Your souls will find rest, for my yoke is easy and my burden light."

Materials: ✓ this picture of a double yoke ✓ a candle and/or incense

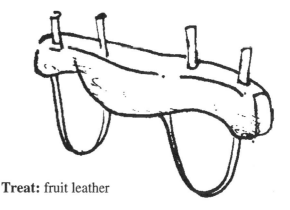

Treat: fruit leather

Leader's Instructions: Gather the family, and light the candle and/or incense. Open with prayer, read the Scripture, and lead the Share and Commit sections.

Share: A yoke is a wooden bar or frame that fits over the heads of two animals so they can work together. Long ago, it was an arched device put on the neck of a person who had been defeated. Both of these kinds of yokes give us insight on Jesus' invitation to take his yoke, as he asks us to work with him and to submit to him.

Let's try a kind of prayer in which we meet Jesus in our imagination. Because Jesus is risen, he is beyond time and space and can be very present to each of us in this prayer.

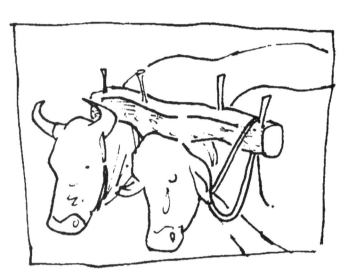

Sit comfortably with your hands in your lap and your eyes closed. Breathe deeply and gently, not loudly, in through your nose and out through your mouth. Continue with this slow deep breathing as you imagine yourself on a grassy hill with a gentle breeze blowing and the sun shining. It is a pleasant place. You start walking downhill...down the hillside slowly...climbing down...farther down...down...down. Eventually, you reach a valley. It's cool there, and the breeze is soft as it makes the colorful wildflowers dance. There is a pathway just in front of you, and you start walking down it. Ahead, you see a figure in a white robe. As you get closer, you see that it's Jesus. You're not really surprised. After all, you were hoping to meet him. Notice how happy he is to see you. He suggests that you stop and rest with him under a nearby tree, where the two of you can talk. As you rest, the two of you see a farmer with two oxen in a yoke pass by. The scene reminds you that you wanted to talk with Jesus about being yoked to him. So you tell him of your concerns, and you ask him questions. (Allow for a silent pause here to give others

time to "talk with Jesus," then continue with the exercise.)

Jesus does not rush you, and for this you are grateful. (Pause again for about another minute of silence.)

It's time to go. Jesus says, "I love you." He suggests that you come back here to talk with him anytime you like, about anything you like. You thank him and get up from the ground to go back up the hill, climbing up, up...up...up...until you're back at the top. At the count of three, open your eyes: 1...2...3.

How do you feel? Was anyone able to imagine the hill and going down it? What did you see and do? (At this point, let each person take a turn sharing whatever he or she liked about the exercise.) Did you get a chance to ask Jesus any questions about being yoked with him? Are there any other concerns you might have about putting his yoke on?

Does it make sense that Jesus' yoke can refresh a person? Are there areas in your life in which Jesus wants you to put on his yoke rather than you going where you want and carrying the burden by yourself?

Commit: Each day this week, let's consider at least one way we can work so closely with Jesus as to be yoked with him.

Altar Sign: Open this book to the picture of the yoke and set it on the altar space as a reminder that Jesus is willing to "pull" with you as you work for God.

Prayer: God of creation, the working animals teach us how to cooperate with you. May we be open to the yoke of Christ that your will may be done in our lives. Amen.

Close: Share a hug, and enjoy your treat.

Fifteenth Sunday in Ordinary Time

▪▪▪▪▪▪

Theme: Why don't we listen to God?

Reading: *Matthew 13:1-9 (Gospel)*
Jesus, on leaving the house on a certain day, sat down by the lakeshore. Such great crowds gathered around him that he went and took his seat in a boat while the crowd stood along the shore. He addressed them at length in parables, speaking in this fashion: "One day a farmer went out sowing. Part of what was sowed landed on a footpath, where birds came and ate it up. Part of it fell on rocky ground, where it had little soil. It sprouted at once since the soil had no depth, but when the sun rose and scorched it, it began to wither for lack of roots. Again, part of the seed fell among thorns, which grew up and choked it. Part of it finally landed on good soil and yielded grain at a hundred- or sixty- or thirtyfold. Let everyone heed what you hear!"

Materials: ✓ bean seeds ✓ a pot with dirt (Note: It is recommended that you go outside by a garden, field, or park for this session. If this is not possible, have a few pots in which plants are already growing and struggling.)

Treat: jelly beans, with or without sugar, as dietary needs indicate (If you do go outside, bring along something to drink.)

Leader's Instructions: This lesson would best be done by a garden, a flower bed in a park, or an open area. Begin with prayer, and then read the Scripture. As you read, point out the footpath, the rocky ground, the thorns, and the good soil around you. Invite everyone to get comfortable on the ground, and lead the Share and Commit sections.

Share: If the farmer is God and the seed is God's word, then we are the ground. Because we listen to God more at some times than at other times, we're probably more than one type of ground. In fact, most people have all of the kinds of soil in them when it comes to listening to God.

The footpath in us might be the times we are not "on track," when we're going our own way without consulting God. The rocky ground in us might be stubbornness and pride that won't let God's way take root in us. The thorns are the worries and temptations that we let grow inside us. The good soil in us is the way we let God's messages make a difference in our lives.

When do you ignore what God wants? When do you tend to be stubborn? What do you worry about? What tempts you away from what God wants for you? When is it easy for you to listen to God? When do you see others ignoring what God wants, being stubborn, or worrying? How can we encourage one another to be good soil?

Commit: This week, let's tell one another when we notice "good soil." Let's also try not to worry, to be stubborn, or to be prideful.

Altar Sign: Plant the bean seeds in a pot and place the pot on the altar space. (Ask someone to be responsible for watering the soil regularly. Tell that person not to pull out any weeds that might grow.) The plant will remind the family to consider what kind of ground they are being each day.

Prayer: Dear God, you are the farmer who has chosen to give us much freedom in how we respond to you. We ask your blessing on us as we strive to be faithful amid the temptations of life. We pray for the grace to be good soil for your word. Amen.

Close: Share a family hug, and pass around the treats and drinks. Take something back with you from the outdoor space you are in: a small pebble, a wildflower, a leaf. Place it on the altar space.

Sixteenth Sunday in Ordinary Time

■ ■ ■ ■ ■ ■

Theme: Tolerance and a little goodness will go far.

Reading: *Matthew 13:24-30, 33 (Gospel)*

Jesus proposed to the crowd another parable: "The reign of God may be likened to one who sowed good seed in a field. While everyone was asleep, the enemy came and sowed weeds through the wheat, then made off. When the crop began to mature and yield grain, the weeds made their appearance as well. The owner's slaves came and said, 'Did you not sow good seed in your field? Where are the weeds coming from?' The owner answered, 'I see an enemy's hand in this.' The slaves then said, 'Do you want us to go out and pull them up?' 'No,' came the reply. 'Pull up the weeds and you might take the wheat along with them. Let them grow together until harvest; then at harvesttime I will order the harvesters to first collect the weeds and bundle them up to burn, and then gather the wheat into my barn.'"

Jesus offered them still another image: "The reign of God is like yeast that a woman took and kneaded into three measures of flour. Eventually, the whole mass of dough began to rise."

Materials: ✓ the pot from last week (It is recommended that you go outside for this session.)

Treat: yeast bread or fresh-made bread (A frozen variety will work fine.)

Leader's Instructions: Prepare the bread ahead of time, unless you are staying at home. If you're conducting this session at home, time the baking to finish as your meeting comes to a close. Gather the family at a garden area or at home with your pot from last week. Open with prayer, read the Scripture, and lead the Share and Commit sections.

Share: Even if you are familiar with the parables, consider the God that the parables tell us about: the owner who tolerates the work of an enemy, the woman who uses a little goodness that has a far-reaching effect.

Are you surprised by these ideas of God? Have you ever experienced God's tolerance of the work of an enemy in your life? Were you glad God was tolerant, that is, did any good eventually come out of it—or do you wish God had set things up differently?

Did you ever see a small act of goodness have a big effect? What lesson did you learn when you saw that small act of goodness have a big effect? Is it hard to give God feminine attributes?

Commit: Let's think about those situations in our own lives that need tolerance or goodness; let's try to bring tolerance or goodness to those situations.

Altar Sign: Place the pot (leave the bits of weeds growing) on the altar space to remind family members to do good, even if it doesn't seem to show or count for much.

Prayer: Dear God, you are like a mother and a father to us. We thank you for your wisdom in setting up the world. Even if we don't understand how or why, we place our trust in you. We pray for the grace to know you fully and to work to make your reign happen on earth. Amen.

Close: Share a hug, and enjoy your treat. Take something back with you from the outdoor space you are in: a small pebble, a wildflower, a leaf. Place it on the altar space.

Seventeenth Sunday in Ordinary Time

■■■■■

Theme: We long to gain the treasure of God.

Reading: *Matthew 13:44-46 (Gospel)*
Jesus said to the crowd: "The reign of God is like a buried treasure that a person found in a field. Hiding it again, and rejoicing at the find, the person went and sold all that was owned in order to buy that field. Or again, the reign of God is like a merchant's search for fine pearls. Upon finding a really valuable one, the merchant went back and put up for sale everything else to be able to buy that pearl."

Materials: ✓ a small, empty wooden chest or jewelry box ✓ different colored diamond-shaped pieces of paper (On each "diamond" write a different word or phrase like "love," "peace," "everlasting life" "saved by Jesus," "comfort," "forgiveness," "communion," "faithfulness.") ✓ blank pieces of diamond-shaped paper ✓ pencils

Treat: foil-wrapped chocolate "coins" or gumballs (sugar-free, if necessary)

Leader's Instructions: Before the meeting, wrap the treats and place them in the chest or jewelry box. On top of them, arrange the pieces of paper—both the blank ones and the ones with words on them. Don't let anyone see what's in the box ahead of time. When it's time to open the box, make a big deal of it being a very special treasure.

Gather the family, open with prayer, and place the jewelry box or "treasure" chest in the center of the group. Don't let anyone open it. Read the Scripture, and lead the Share and Commit sections.

Share: What do you think we might find if we opened a person's jewelry box or a pirate's treasure chest? How would these things help you now and forever?

What do you think we might find if we opened God's jewelry box or treasure chest? How might those things help you now and forever?

Now, we're going to open this "treasure" chest. (Remember, make a big deal of this part.) Are you ready? Are you sure? Any guesses about what we might find here? (Listen to the guesses anyone wants to offer. Be prepared for some comments of disappointment once you open the box.)

Okay, let's open our treasure chest. Ah, let's see. What's this? (Look at each diamond-shaped paper. Talk about that particular "treasure.") What might a person have to do away with to gain this treasure? Would it be worth it to you?

Can anyone think of a "treasure" that isn't mentioned on these diamonds? (Ask someone to write those "treasures" on the blank diamonds and place them in the box with the others.)

Commit: This week, let's try to choose God's "treasures" instead of the world's.

Altar Sign: Place the open box with all the diamond papers inside on the altar space to remind the family of the wonderful "treasure" that awaits them—a "treasure" they cannot see with just the human eye alone.

Prayer: Dear God, keeper of all the treasures in heaven and on earth, we thank you for the treasure of Jesus and one another. We pray for the courage to give up those things that take us from you and for the boldness to seek all the treasures you have to offer. Amen.

Close: Unwrap the treats, and share them—and a family hug.

Eighteenth Sunday in Ordinary Time
■ ■ ■ ■ ■

Theme: Jesus cares about us—his people.

Reading: *Matthew 14:13-21 (Gospel)*
When Jesus heard of the death of John the Baptist, he withdrew by boat to a deserted place by himself. The crowds heard of it and followed him on foot from the towns. When he disembarked and saw the vast throng, his heart was moved with pity, and he cured their sick.

As evening drew on, his disciples came to him with the suggestion: "This is a deserted place and it is already late. Dismiss the crowds so that they may go to the villages and buy some food for themselves." Jesus said to them: "There is no need for them to disperse. Give them something to eat yourselves." "We have nothing here," they replied, "but five loaves of bread and a couple of fish." "Bring them here," Jesus said. Then he ordered the crowds to sit down on the grass. He took the five loaves and two fish, looked up to heaven, blessed and broke them and gave the loaves to the disciples, who in turn gave them to the people. All those present ate their fill. The fragments that remained, when gathered up, filled twelve baskets. The men who ate numbered five thousand; women and children were too numerous to count.

Materials: ✓ pieces of paper cut in the shape of a fish (enough for each person to have several) ✓ crayons and/or pencils

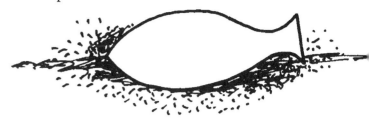

Treat: pancakes or waffles together (prepared together at the end of the session)

Leader's Instructions: Gather the family, open with prayer, and explain that the reading for today tells about how Jesus took pity on people's immediate needs, caring for them and feeding them. Read the Scripture, and lead the Share and Commit sections.

Share: Have you ever wanted some peace and quiet but someone came along who really needed you, so you gave him or her some time? Did you ever need someone to give you some time?

What are the kinds of daily needs that other people meet, which we tend to take for granted? Like who does the cooking, mows the lawn, and does the laundry and cleaning around here? Who pays the bills, earns the money, washes the car, does the shopping? As a form of thanking that person for caring as Jesus did, write on a fish what it was that he or she did, then give it to the person. Even if the person isn't here right now; we'll see to it that the person gets it.

This Scripture is about people eating together. There is great power in eating together; when you eat with someone, you begin to feel like friends. For example, at school, kids like to eat with their friends. When there's a new student at school, asking that person to sit at the table with you is a gesture of friendliness. How often do we as a family eat together at home, around a table, without the TV or radio on? (Note: it does not have to be the evening meal.) Are we satisfied with the frequency? How could schedules be adjusted to make a meal together happen more often?

What might we do as a family to meet another's needs, particularly regarding food?

Commit: This week, let's come together for meals more than we usually do. Let's also try to meet another's need for food.

Altar Sign: Place the fish on the altar space as a visible "thank you" for those things often taken for granted. Let them serve as a reminder to say "thank you" more often.

Prayer: Dear God, you are the creator of the world and all that we have. We thank you for the care Jesus showed to us and for the people who continue that loving care today. Open our hearts to be more loving and caring toward those we live with and those we meet. Amen.

Close: Share a hug, and then make the treat.

Nineteenth Sunday in Ordinary Time
▪▪▪▪▪▪

Theme: We step out in faith.

Reading: *Matthew 14:22-33 (Gospel)*
After the crowds had their fill, Jesus insisted that his disciples get into the boat and precede him to the other side. When he had sent them away, he went up on the mountain by himself to pray, remaining there alone as evening drew on. Meanwhile the boat, already several hundred yards out from shore, was being tossed about in the waves raised by strong headwinds. At about three in the morning, he came walking toward them on the lake. When the disciples saw him walking on the water, they were terrified. "It is a ghost!" they said, and in their fear they began to cry out. Jesus hastened to reassure them: "Get hold of yourselves! It is I. Do not be afraid!" Peter spoke up and said, "Lord, if it is really you, tell me to come to you across the water." "Come!" Jesus said. So Peter got out of the boat and began to walk on the water, moving toward Jesus. But when he perceived how strong the wind was, becoming fright-

ened he began to sink, and cried out, "Lord, save me!" Jesus at once stretched out his hand and caught Peter. "How little faith you have!" he exclaimed. "Why did you falter?"

Once they had climbed into the boat, the wind died down. Those who were in the boat showed him reverence, declaring, "Beyond doubt you are the Son of God."

Materials: ✓ ice-cream sticks (enough for everyone to have ten or more) ✓ glue ✓ crayons or markers ✓ strong scissors ✓ one piece of paper per person (optional)

Treat: Popsicles™

Leader's Instructions: Gather the family, and open with prayer. Read the Scripture, and lead the Share and Commit sections.

Share: Peter was willing to step out in faith, and for a moment, he succeeded. It was hard for him to keep faith in his ability, but he still trusted in God's love for him. As we each make a boat with these ice-cream sticks, let's think about times we find it easy to trust and times when we find it hard to trust. (Some may find "building" the boat easier by gluing the sticks on a sheet of paper.)

When is it easier for you to trust God? When is faith in God harder? What do you tend to do when your faith level is low? Are you satisfied with that? Is there some way you would like to respond to God, some service you would like to do, but you're afraid to get "out of the boat"? What is it that keeps you from stepping out in faith? What is the spiritual gift you need from God? Write it on your boat and "christen" your boat. Name it *Courage* or *Patience*, depending on the special spiritual gift you need.

Commit: This week, let's each make a special effort to step out in faith in some way.

Altar Sign: Place the "christened" boats on the altar space to remind the family to trust in God even when they feel like they're about to "go under."

Prayer: Gentle God, you know our wobbly and weak faith. We thank you for your patience with us. We pray for the grace to be ever more trusting in you. Amen.

Close: Take turns admiring one another's boats, and then enjoy your treat.

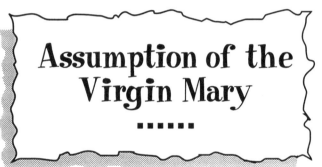

Assumption of the Virgin Mary

Theme: Let our being proclaim the greatness of God!

Reading: *Luke 1:39-56 (Gospel)*
Mary set out, proceeding in haste into the hill country to a town of Judah, where she entered the house of Zechariah and greeted Elizabeth. When Elizabeth heard Mary's greeting, the baby leapt in her womb. Elizabeth was filled with the Holy Spirit and cried out in a loud voice: "Blest are you among women and blest is the fruit of your womb. But who am I that the mother of my Savior should come to me? The moment your greeting sounded in my ears, the baby leapt in my womb for joy. Blest is she who trusted that God's words to her would be fulfilled."

Then Mary said: "My being proclaims the greatness of God, my spirit finds joy in God my savior for God has looked upon this servant in her lowliness; all ages to come shall call me blessed. God who is mighty has done great things for me, holy is God's name; God's mercy is from age to age on those who show reverence.

"God has shown power and might and has confused the proud in their inmost thoughts. God has deposed the mighty from their thrones and raised the lowly to high places. The hungry have been given every good thing while the rich have been sent away empty. God has upheld the servant Israel, ever mindful of eternal mercy; even as God promised our ancestors, promised Abraham, Sarah, and all their descendants forever."

Mary remained with Elizabeth about three months and then returned home.

Materials: ✓ any book about the lives of the saints ✓ 30 or more streamers of crepe paper or white paper (cut in strips 1 to 3 feet long by 4 inches wide) ✓ markers or crayons ✓ one rubber band

Treat: variety of candies or nuts in a bag or plastic wrap, tied with a ribbon (one small bag for each person)

Leader's Instructions: Prepare the treat bags and streamers ahead of time. Gather the family together, open with prayer, read the Scripture, and lead the Share and Commit sections.

Share: Mary saw God's goodness not only to her but through the centuries, and she was so filled with love of God and holiness that she couldn't hide it. It shined from her. Today, we remember Mary and others in our faith family whose lives proclaimed God's greatness.

What makes Mary so great? (Ask someone to write the traits or virtues that are mentioned, one on each streamer, and write Mary's name on the other side.)

Who are some saints we can think of, and what did they do that showed God's greatness? (If any of these traits or virtues are the same as Mary's, put that saint's name next to Mary's on the same streamer. If it's a new virtue, start a new strip. Use the book on the saints, if needed.)

Which of our family members—grandparents, great-grandparents, aunts, uncles, cousins, and so forth—have shown God's goodness? How? (If any of these traits or virtues have been mentioned, add that person's name to the streamer. If traits or virtues haven't been mentioned, make a new streamer.)

Who proclaims God's goodness today—people we know? How? (Add their names or make new streamers.)

People whose lives proclaim God's goodness brighten the world, just as these colorful strips do. There have been many people we know or know about who have done much to brighten our lives and the world. We are blessed to remember them.

What did it require of these people in order for them to become the light they are today? What does it mean for us in our lives? How can we encourage one another to live lives that proclaim God's goodness?

Commit: This week, let's remember the faith of others. Let's model our lives after theirs as we proclaim God's goodness and greatness.

Altar Sign: Hold all the streamers by one end and wrap a rubber band around the end. Place this on the altar space or hang it from a hook or pin on the wall. Let it remind the family of God's goodness showing in the world.

Prayer: Glorious God, you chose Mary and honored her faithfulness. We celebrate that this week, and ask your blessing on our lives. We pray for the grace to respond to you every day in ways that will proclaim your greatness to the world. Amen.

Close: If it is a breezy day, "fly" the streamers outside. Enjoy your treat, and give one another a hug.

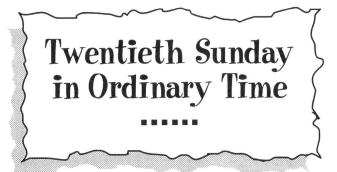

Twentieth Sunday in Ordinary Time

Theme: A different perspective can change hearts.

Reading: *Matthew 15:21-28 (Gospel)*
Jesus withdrew to the district of Tyre and Sidon. It happened that a Canaanite woman living in that locality presented herself, crying out to him, "Lord, Son of David, have pity on me! My daughter is terribly troubled by a demon." He gave her no word of response. His disciples came up and began to entreat him, "Get rid of her. She keeps shouting after us." "My mission is only to the lost sheep of the house of Israel," Jesus replied. She came forward then and did him homage with the plea, "Help me, Lord!" But he answered, "It is not right to take the food of sons and daughters and throw it to the dogs." "Please, Lord," she insisted, "even the dogs eat the leavings that fall from their masters' tables." Jesus then said in reply, "Woman, you have great faith!" Your wish will come to pass." That very moment her daughter got better.

Materials: ✓ a prism or a container of water (This session is best conducted outdoors.)

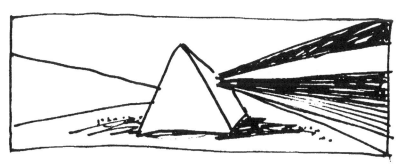

Treat: juice frozen in ice-cube trays

Leader's Instructions: If at all possible, hold this session outside in the sun, with either your prism or your container of water. Gather the family, and open with prayer. Read the Scripture. Ask family members to watch how the light changes color and shape as the prism turns or as they slowly move their gaze across the water's surface. Lead the Share and Commit sections.

Share: See how the light changes as we change the angle of observation? In the same way, we can change our perspective about people.

Do you think the Canaanite woman was too bold, or was Jesus unusually rude? Do you think that the Canaanite woman was not too bold and that Jesus was not unusually rude? Have you ever judged someone based on the religion he or she practiced or didn't practice, or on where he or she came from—only to realize later that your first impression was a mistake? Has anyone ever judged you in the same way?

Have you ever felt like you should give someone or something a second chance? What helps you decide if offering a second chance is an idea inspired by God? Does everyone, every time, deserve a second chance? Why? If you choose not to offer a second chance, does that mean you should hold a grudge? How might the family help you in this?

Commit: This week, let's be especially patient and thoughtful of certain people in certain situations.

Altar Sign: Hang the prism near the altar space, or place the container of water on the altar space. Let the changing lights remind family members that their understanding of what God desires might need to be corrected. (Don't use glass items on the altar; someone may drink the water.)

Prayer: Good God, you desire to give everyone everything he or she needs. May we help you by not excluding individuals or groups of people. May hurts that we have experienced when we were excluded be healed. We pray that all people may be united as one family. Amen.

Close: Share a hug with the family, splash (gently!) one another with water, and enjoy the treat.

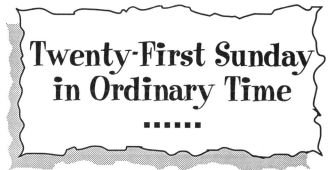

Twenty-First Sunday in Ordinary Time
■■■■■■

Theme: Who is Jesus to us?

Reading: *Matthew 16:13-20 (Gospel)*
When Jesus came to the neighborhood of Caesarea Philippi, he asked his disciples this question: "Who do people say that the Son of Man is?" They replied, "Some say John the Baptist, others Elijah, still others Jeremiah or one of the prophets." "And you," Jesus said to them, "who do you say that I am?" "You are the Messiah," Simon Peter answered, "the Son of the living God!" Jesus replied, "Blest are you, Simon son of John! No mere human has revealed this to you, but our heavenly God. I, for my part, declare to you, you are 'Rock,' and on this rock I will build my church, and the jaws of death shall not prevail against it. I will entrust to you the keys of the reign of God. Whatever you declare bound on earth shall be bound in heaven; whatever you declare loosed on earth shall be loosed in heaven." Then Jesus strictly ordered his disciples not to tell anyone that he was the Messiah.

Materials: ✓ a white or light-colored poster board (or a large sheet of freezer paper) ✓ crayons and/or markers

Treat: freezer pops (variety of colors)

Leader's Instructions: Gather the family, place the materials in the middle of the gathering, and open with prayer. Read the Scripture, and lead the Share and Commit sections.

Share: In each of our lives there comes a time when we are put on the spot and must say, out loud or by our actions, who we believe Jesus is. We're going to make a project using words, pictures, symbols, or anything else to describe who we think Jesus is today.

Select a small portion of the poster to be your "spot." In that space, draw something that makes a statement about who you think Jesus is today. (Allow time for each person to carefully plan a drawing. Once everyone is through or close to it, have each person explain what he or she drew or wrote and why.)

If we had done this poster one year ago, or five years ago, would it have been different? How? What causes a person's understanding of Jesus to grow? What causes a person's knowledge in any subject area to grow?

Is there anything you would like to do to get to know Jesus better? How can the family support you in this?

Commit: Each day this week, let's take a special period of quiet time to be with Jesus, to think about who he is.

Altar Sign: Place the poster on the altar space or tape it to the wall nearby so everyone might be enriched by all the images of Jesus that he or she thought about.

Prayer: Holy God, we desire to know your Son fully, because if we know Jesus, we know you better too. May we be blessed with eyes that see Jesus' presence around us. May we be filled with joy and hope. Amen.

Close: Have someone take a picture of you and your family holding the poster board (optional). Take a few minutes to admire your work together, share a hug, and enjoy your treats.

Twenty-Second Sunday in Ordinary Time

Theme: What good is it if we gain the whole world and lose ourselves?

Reading: *Matthew 16:21-27 (Gospel)*
From then on, Jesus started to indicate to his disciples that he must go to Jerusalem to suffer greatly at the hands of the elders, the chief priests, and the scribes, be put to death, and raised up on the third day. At this, Peter took him aside and began to remonstrate with him. "May you be spared! God forbid that any such thing ever happen to you!" Jesus turned on Peter and said, "Get out of my sight, you satan! You are trying to make me trip and fall. You are not judging by God's standards but by human."

Jesus then said to his disciples: "If any of you wish to come after me, you must deny your very self, take up your cross, and begin to follow in my footsteps. You who would save your life will lose it, but you who lose your life for my sake will find it. What profit would you show if you were to gain the whole world and ruin yourself in the process? What can you offer in exchange for your very self? The Son of Man will come with God's glory accompanied by the angels. When he does, he will repay each of you according to your conduct."

Materials: ✓ catalogs and/or magazines with items of interest to those gathered ✓ a Bible (with pictures for young children) ✓ binoculars and/or a magnifying glass (optional) ✓ orange peelings kept in one long strip (optional)

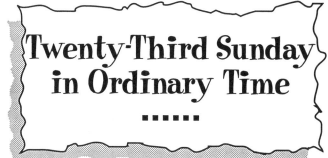

Treat:
an orange for each person (Note: Invite everyone to try to peel the orange in one long strip. This signifies the emptiness of losing oneself.)

Leader's Instructions: Gather the family, open with prayer, and read the Scripture. Place the catalogs and/or magazines in the middle of the group, and lead the Share and Commit sections.

Share: Imagine that you can have anything and everything you want. Look through these magazines and catalogs. What would you pick? Would having ALL these things lead you closer to God or distract you from God? How and why? Would having SOME of these things lead you closer to God or distract you from God? How and why? Would having NONE of these things lead you closer to God or distract you from God? How do we avoid using things to prove that we are "somebody"? Would you consider this a complete description of yourself: "I am a child of God"? Why or why not?

How can you tell when your focus has shifted away from God and toward having things? What do you do to get the focus back on God? How can the family help you in this?

Commit: This week, let's ask God to help us find a good balance between having things and following God.

Altar Sign: Place the Bible on the altar space as a reminder of where you will find true happiness. If you have binoculars or a magnifying glass, place it on the altar space as well, to remind you to focus on God.

Prayer: Blessed God, you care so much about us that you warn us about the dangers of what will take us from you. May we pay attention. May we focus our attention on you so the things of this world lose their appeal. Amen.

Close: Take turns with the binoculars or magnifying glass, focusing on God's creation. Share a hug with all, and enjoy your treat.

Twenty-Third Sunday in Ordinary Time
■■■■■■

Theme: Genuine love has the willingness to correct and accept correction.

Reading: *Matthew 18:15-20 (Gospel)*
Jesus said to his disciples: "If your sister or brother should commit some wrong against you, go and point out the fault, but keep it between the two of you. If she or he does not listen, however, summon another so every case may stand on the word of two or three witnesses. If you are ignored, refer it to the Church. If your brother or sister ignores even the Church, then treat that one as you would a Gentile or a tax collector. I assure you, whatever you declare bound on earth shall be held bound in heaven, and whatever you declare loosed on earth shall be held loosed in heaven.

"Again I tell you, if two of you join your voices on earth to pray for anything, whatever, it shall be granted you by my Father in heaven. Where two or three are gathered in my name, there am I in their midst."

Materials: ✓ paper (two sheets per person) ✓ pencils ✓ crayons

Treat: broken cookies (Nobody's perfect!)

Leader's Instructions: Gather the family, and open with prayer. After reading the Scripture, lead the Share and Commit sections.

Share: Being corrected is a very hard thing for many of us to accept because we generally want everyone to think well of us. Correction is especially hard if it's delivered with name-calling like "You're stupid" or "You're clumsy." (If your family does not already have a rule about how people tell others what's wrong, make that rule now. "No name-calling in this family. Just tell the person what you don't like, why you don't like it, and what you want him or her to do instead.") When we are corrected, our response should be respectful: "Oops, I'm sorry. I won't do it again" is a nice polite response.

Have you ever been corrected by someone who yelled at you and called you names? How did you feel about that? Did it make you want to change or please the other person?

Have you ever been corrected calmly and quietly, with "just the facts"? How did you feel about that? Were you more inclined to listen?

On a scale of one to ten—one being very easy and ten being very hard—how hard is it for you to accept correction? Do you like to pretend that you are perfect? Do you want others to think you're perfect? Does God think you are perfect? Does God love you just the way you are? Have you ever felt the freedom that comes from being able to make a mistake, get corrected, and not get "down" on yourself?

Because humor is one way for us to keep from taking mistakes too seriously, we're going to draw a cartoon of ourselves making a mistake, using the "Oops—sorry!" approach. Share your cartoon with others when you're finished.

Commit: This week, let's be more patient with ourselves and others when mistakes are made. Let's accept correction with courtesy and gratitude.

Altar Sign: Place the cartoons on the altar space as a sign of everyone's willingness to accept gentle correction in the spirit of love.

Prayer: Dear Jesus, you know how to guide and correct, even as you treat us gently. We pray for the grace to treat ourselves as gently, but as firmly, as you treat us. Amen.

Close: Admire each other's cartoons, and try not to take offense if others say you are "right on target." Share a hug and the treat.

Twenty-Fourth Sunday in Ordinary Time

■ ■ ■ ■ ■ ■

Theme: We forgive, even if the other is wrong.

Reading: *Matthew 18:21-35 (Gospel)*
Peter came up and asked Jesus, "Lord, when my brother or sister wrongs me, how often must I forgive? Seven times?" "No," Jesus replied, "not seven times; I say seventy times seven times. That is why the reign of God may be said to be like a ruler who wanted to settle accounts with the officials. Beginning the auditing, one was brought in who owed the ruler a huge amount. Having no way to pay, the ruler ordered him to be sold, along with his wife, his children, and all his property, in payment of the debt, as was the custom. At that, the official paid homage and begged, 'Be patient with me and I will pay you back in full!' Moved with pity, the ruler let the official go and completely wrote off the debt.

"But when that same official went out, he met a fellow servant who owed him a mere fraction of what he had owed the ruler. The official seized his fellow servant. 'Pay back what you owe,' he demanded. The other servant dropped to his knees and began to plead, 'Just give me time and I will pay you back in full.' But the first fellow would hear none of it. Instead, he had his fellow servant put in jail until he paid back what he owed. When the other servants saw what had happened, they were badly shaken and went to the ruler to report the whole incident.

"The ruler sent for the first official and said, 'You worthless wretch! I canceled your entire debt when you pleaded with me. Should you not have dealt mercifully with your fellow servant as I dealt with you?' Then in anger, the ruler handed the first official

over to the torturers until he paid back all he owed. God in heaven will treat you in exactly the same way unless each of you forgives your brother or sister from your heart."

Materials: ✓ several lemons (or one lemon and packs of unsweetened lemonade mix, with the sugar or sweetener measured ahead of time in a small bowl) ✓ small spoon

Treat: lemonade and either cookies, popcorn, or pretzels

Leader's Instruction: Prepare the lemonade ahead of time, without sweetener. Instead, have the sugar or sweetener in a bowl next to the pitcher of lemonade. Place a spoon in the sugar or sweetener. Gather the family, open with a prayer, read the Scripture, and lead the Share and Commit sections.

Share: There is a saying, "If life gives you lemons, make lemonade." We can't do this unless we are like the ruler who, when someone asked him for mercy, he had it to offer. We can't sweeten the lemons of our lives if we refuse mercy to others, hold a grudge, or notice every little wrong that everyone does. This does not mean that the other person is right, or that we'll stop working to change a situation. It does mean that we are willing to forgive.

Think of what a family member, a friend, a person at work or school, a neighbor, or a trusted peer "owes" you in terms of favors or forgiveness. If you are willing to "wipe the slate clean," say so now. (Each time a person mentions someone he or she plans to forgive, put some of the sweetener into the pitcher of lemonade. Continue with "debts" being forgiven until all of the sweetener you previously measured has been used.)

Commit: This week, let's try to forgive as much as possible. Let's try to let go of all grudges.

Altar Sign: Place one whole lemon on the altar space as a sign of the constant potential for life to sour you, and your potential to sweeten life with forgiveness.

Prayer: Merciful God, you have forgiven our sins over and over and over. Some might think it foolish to do as you have done. We pray for the courage to forgive and the wisdom to act when a wrongful situation continues. Amen.

Close: Share a hug with each family member, and enjoy the sweet lemonade with the treat of your choice.

Twenty-Fifth Sunday in Ordinary Time
∎ ∎ ∎ ∎ ∎

Theme: God's generosity is beyond our imagination.

Reading: *Matthew 20:1-16 (Gospel)*
Jesus told his disciples this parable: "The reign of God is like the case of the owner of an estate who went out at dawn to hire workers for the vineyard. After reaching an agreement with them, the owner sent them out to work. About midmorning the owner came out and saw others standing around the marketplace without work, so he said to them, 'You, too, go

along to my vineyard and I will pay you whatever is fair.' At that, they went away. Again around noon and midafternoon the owner came out and did the same. Finally, going out in the late afternoon the owner found still others standing around. To these the owner said, 'Why have you been standing here idle all day?' 'No one has hired us,' they replied. 'You go to the vineyard too.'

"When evening came the owner of the vineyard said to the foreman, 'Call the workers and give them their pay, but begin with the last group and end with the first.' When those hired late in the afternoon came up they received a full day's pay, and when the first group appeared they supposed they would get more; yet they received the same daily wage. Thereupon they complained to the owner, 'This last group did only an hour's work, but you have put them on the same basis as we who have worked a full day in the scorching heat.' 'My friend,' the owner said to one in reply, 'I do you no injustice. You agreed on the usual wage, did you not? Take your pay and go home. I intend to give this worker who was hired last the same pay as you. I am free to do as I please with my money, am I not? Or are you envious because I am generous?' Thus the last shall be first and the first shall be last."

Materials: ✓ a box of candy, with sugar or dietary (Use the following formula to determine how many pieces of candy you will need: the age of the oldest child times the number of people in the family. For example, if the oldest child is twelve years old and there are five people in the family, you will need sixty pieces of candy.) ✓ a sheet of paper with GOD IS GENEROUS written on it

Treat: the candy pieces as described above

Leader's Instructions: Before you begin, review the last part of Share. You will need to be familiar with counting out the pieces of candy to make the point about generosity and fairness.

Gather the family, and place the bag of candy in the center of the gathering. Begin with an opening prayer, read the Scripture, and lead the Share and Commit sections.

Share: Was the owner of the vineyard fair or not? (Let those gathered discuss this for a few minutes.)

Sometimes it is hard to understand people's generosity. Sometimes people's generosity actually seems foolish. Imagine, for instance, that I were to give __(name of oldest child)__ here ____ pieces of candy since she(he) is __(age of oldest child)__ years old. (Count out that many pieces of candy and give them to the oldest child.) Would she(he) be glad? Now, suppose I decide to give __(name of another child)__ the same amount of candy, and __(name of anyone else in the family)__ the same too. (Continue to mention all those present and count out the same amount of candy to each.) Is that fair? Some may think so; some may not think so. Now, if I decided to divide the candy in a different way, I might not have enough for everyone. Sooner or later, the candy is going to run out—and most of the time, someone is going to think that my way of dividing it isn't fair.

But God's love, forgiveness, and blessings aren't like that. God is willing to give to anyone at anytime; God doesn't run out of love, forgiveness, and blessings. Do you think that's good? Do you feel jealous sometimes when it looks like someone has received an abundance of goodness and it looks like you didn't? What if you were sure that God would give you all you need, whenever you needed it? What are the ways God is generous to us right now? (Ask someone to write the responses on the sheet of paper marked GOD IS GENEROUS.)

Commit: This week, let's think carefully and gratefully about all that God has given to us with love. Let's also be happy with and for others in their good fortune.

Altar Sign: Place the GOD IS GENEROUS paper on the altar space to remind the family that God will give them all they need. Add responses to the list during the week, as desired.

Prayer: Gracious God, your desire to give is unending, and we are glad. We pray for the grace to always respond to you in love and to rejoice with our brothers and sisters on earth. Amen.

Close: Divide the candy again, if necessary, and share hugs as everyone enjoys theirs.

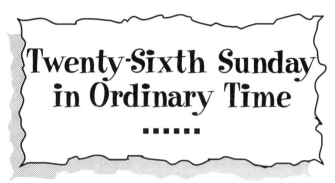

Twenty-Sixth Sunday in Ordinary Time
■■■■■

Theme: We want to say what we mean.

Reading: *Matthew 21:28-32 (Gospel)*
Jesus said to the chief priests and elders of the people: "What do you think of this case? There was a parent with two children. The parent approached the older child and said, 'Go out and work in the vineyard today.' The older child replied, 'I am on my way'; but never went. Then the parent came to the younger child and said the same thing. This child said in reply, 'No, I will not'; but afterward regretted it and went. Which of the two did what the parent wanted?" They said, "The second." Jesus said to them, "Let me make it clear that tax collectors and prostitutes are seeing the reign of God before you. When John came preaching a way of holiness, you put no faith in him; but the tax collectors and prostitutes did believe in him. Yet even when you saw that, you did not repent and believe in him."

Materials: ✓ six half-sheets of paper with one of the following statements written on each:

- "No, you can't make me."
- "It's not my job."
- "Why do I have to?"
- "Okay! Okay!"
- "Yes, I hear you."
- "I'm going, I'm going."

✓ six straws to serve as sign holders ✓ enough additional straws for each person's treats

Treat: pixie stix or milk shakes to drink with a straw

Leader's Instructions: Tape a straw to the back of each sheet of paper to make six "signs" that can be held up. Gather the family, and open with prayer. Put the signs within the family circle, and read the Scripture. Lead the Share and Commit sections.

Share: Which of the two do you tend to do: break promises or refuse to make a promise in the first place and then regret it? Have you ever said "Yes" just to please someone or to get him or her to leave you alone? How did you feel about saying "Yes"? What did you want to say instead?

Have you ever said "No" out of stubbornness or spite and wished you hadn't? How did you feel then? What would you like to have said instead? Is it ever all right to say "No" to God? Is it ever all right to say "No" to your parent or another adult? How about to a friend? When is it wrong to say "Yes" to someone? Is it ever wrong to say "Yes" to God?

Commit: This week, let's speak honestly and directly about what we feel and what we want to do. Let's be sure to do what we say we will do.

Altar Sign: Place the signs on the altar space as a reminder not to use those phrases!

Prayer: God of honesty and truth, sometimes we are too tired or too anxious to please that we say what we don't mean and get in trouble. We pray for the courage to be honest and to accept the consequences of that honesty. Amen.

Close: Give one another an honest hug, and enjoy your treat.

Twenty-Seventh Sunday in Ordinary Time
■ ■ ■ ■ ■ ■

Theme: We direct our thoughts to all that is good.

Reading: *Philippians 4:6-9 (Reading II)*
Dismiss all anxiety from your minds. Present your needs to God in every form of prayer and in petitions full of gratitude. Then God's own peace, which is beyond all understanding, will stand guard over your hearts and minds, in Christ Jesus.

Finally, my brothers and sisters, your thoughts should be wholly directed to all that is true, all that deserves respect, all that is honest, pure, admirable, decent, virtuous, or worthy of praise. Live according to what you have learned and accepted, what you have heard me say and seen me do. Then will the God of peace be with you.

Materials: ✓ half a poster board (or an oversized pice of paper) with a large arrow drawn on it (Color the arrow if you wish.) ✓ pencils

Treat: popcorn

Leader's Instructions: Gather the family, and open with prayer. Read the Scripture, and lead the Share and Commit sections.

Share: Have you ever tried to direct your thoughts? Try this: close your eyes, think of a purple and green spotted dinosaur atop a palm tree, jumping rope, and eating bananas. See? Your mind can think of almost anything you ask. So you see, you must be very careful about what goes into your mind. Otherwise, you could easily be distracted from focusing on a Christian life.

Does the music you listen to have words that are about respect for others and love of God? If not, what are the words about? How much of the music you listen to is spiritually healthy for you? Do the TV shows you watch (cartoons and football games included) direct your thoughts to respect others, to decency, to purity, and to that which is worthy of praise? How about commercials?

Many people say that TV shows and movies do not influence their thinking or behavior. They say that what's going on in the show or in the movie is wrong; they say that they know the commercials are just using bodies to sell products. However, once a picture is in our minds, it remains. When it is seen over and over, it becomes normal; we begin to see stuff that is indecent, impure, and disrespectful as normal—even funny.

Do the books and magazines you read increase your love of God and respect for all people? Why spend time on something that will not lead you to God, but instead, leads to temptation?

What do you need to do about your listening, watching, and reading habits? How can the family support you in this? How will you deal with friends who may question your change in behavior? What will you do when the bad habits of others tempt you to do the same? (Ask someone to write the responses on the "arrow" poster.)

Many families are rediscovering the fun of playing board games or nonbetting card games instead of watching TV. Other families are beginning to read more Christian material and listen to music that has a Christian theme.

Commit: This week, let's look for purity and respect in everything as it goes into our minds.

Altar Sign: Prop the "arrow" poster on the altar or tape it to the wall near the altar space to remind the family to ask themselves, *Are my activities directing my mind and heart to God?*

Prayer: Heavenly God, you made our minds so powerful. We are able to learn and know and create so much. We thank you and ask for your guidance that we might always choose to put good into our minds. Amen.

Close: Share the treat and a family hug. If you have time, play a board game.

Twenty-Eighth Sunday in Ordinary Time

■ ■ ■ ■ ■ ■

Theme: We don't want to be too busy to think about eternity.

Reading: *Matthew 22:1-10 (Gospel)*

Jesus began to address the chief priests and elders of the people, once more using parables. "The reign of God may be likened to a king who gave a wedding banquet for his son. He dispatched the servants to summon the invited guests to the wedding, but they refused to come. A second time he sent other servants, saying: 'Tell those who were invited. See, I have my dinner prepared! My bullocks and cornfed cattle are killed; everything is ready. Come to the feast.' Some ignored the invitation and went their way, one to farm, another to his business. The rest laid hold of the servants, insulted them, and killed them. At this, the king grew furious and sent his army to destroy those murderers and burn their city. Then he said to his servants: 'The banquet is ready, but those who were invited were unfit to come. That is why you must go out into the byroads and invite to the wedding anyone you come upon.' The servants then went out into the byroads and rounded up everyone they met, bad as well as good. This filled the wedding hall with banqueters."

Materials: ✓ typing paper or blank paper for the invitations (If you have a very large family, make one invitation for the entire family, being sure to mention each person by name. Smaller families should issue one invitation per person.) ✓ RSVP note cards or index cards (one per person) ✓ pens ✓ pencils ✓ crayons

Treat: cake (Carrot or pumpkin would be seasonal.)

Leader's Instructions: Prepare the invitations ahead of time. The wording should read something like this:

Dear _____,

You are wholeheartedly invited to spend eternity with me, your God. Don't be alarmed. I have wonderful and marvelous plans for us—and for all my friends here in heaven. I know just how you would want to spend "forever." All your needs will be fulfilled. Please let me know that you will prepare to join us.

With everlasting love,
God

Gather the family, open with prayer, read the Scripture, pass around the invitations, and lead the Share and Commit sections.

Share: If you were invited to a very important party, wouldn't you spend some time deciding what to wear, how to behave, how you would get there?

The big party for followers of God will be in heaven, so we need to consider how ready we are and what else we might be needing to do to get more prepared. For example, what is it in your relationship with God that needs attention? What about your interaction with your brothers and sisters all over the earth? What about yourself? Do you need to take better care of yourself? Do you need to discipline yourself about certain habits and behaviors?

Use the RSVP note cards to respond to God. You might write something like, "Dear God, thanks for the invitation! I can hardly wait! This is what I know I have to do to get ready...." List the special things you have to do.

Share your RSVP note cards with the family, if you would like. How can we support one another as we get ready for God's big party?

Commit: This week, let's do at least one thing that we know will help us get ready for life with God.

Altar Sign: Place on the altar an invitation and the RSVP cards to remind everyone to do what is necessary every day to prepare for eternity with God.

Prayer: Mighty God, sometimes it is too much to believe that you would want us to be with you always. We pray for the grace to see in ourselves what is offensive to you and to cleanse that part of ourselves. We ask to be transformed into your image, in which we were first made. Amen.

Close: Share a hug, and wish one another well in preparing for life with God. Enjoy your treat.

Materials: ✓ an American flag (or a map of the world or a picture of the solar system) ✓ a Bible ✓ a blank sheet of paper

Twenty-Ninth Sunday in Ordinary Time
■ ■ ■ ■ ■ ■

Theme: Which comes first: God or country?

Reading: *Matthew 22:15-21 (Gospel)*
The Pharisees went off and began to plot how they might trap Jesus in speech. They sent their disciples to him, accompanied by Herodian sympathizers, who said: "Teacher, we know you are a truthful man and sincerely teach God's way. You court no one's favor and do not act out of human respect. Give us your opinion, then, in this case. Is it lawful to pay tax to the emperor or not?"

Jesus recognized their bad faith and said to them, "Why are you trying to trip me up, you hypocrites? Show me the coin used for the tax." When they handed him a small Roman coin he asked them, "Whose head is this, and whose inscription?" "Caesar's," they replied. At that, he said to them, "Then give to Caesar what is Caesar's, but give to God what is God's."

Treat: a snack from your country of ancestry

Leader's Instructions: Gather the family, place the materials in the center of the family circle, open with prayer, read the Scripture, and lead the Share and Commit sections.

Share: We don't have Caesar anymore, but we do have our country and government to which we pledge our loyalty and support. However, not everything about our country is right. Today, we're going to think about how to follow God within our democracy.

Is it all right to disagree with the laws, wars, and spending habits of our country? Is it possible to still love our country while disagreeing with the people who make decisions about it? What does the slogan "America—love it or leave it" imply? What would God have to say about this slogan?

How should a Christian decide if he or she should give allegiance to God or to the country when a law is passed that goes against his or her values? In a democracy, one has the right to complain, speak out, write letters to ask for changes, vote, run for office, object conscientiously, protest, and pray. In fact, these are just a few things that people in a democracy can do. Which of these should a Christian do if he or she thinks a law or ruling is wrong? Which of these might you want to do in such a case?

Make a list of some of the issues in our country today that are confusing. In which of these do you think God would overrule "Caesar"? There might be some difference of opinion here. Be tolerant. God does not force anyone to take a certain position; neither should we. Make your reasons known and pray for wisdom. Do you know what the Church teaches about each of these issues? Might you or the family be willing to find out the Church's teaching on these issues?

Commit: Let's commit to doing something about the laws and practices of our country when we feel they go against God's desire.

Altar Sign: Place the flag, map, and/or picture on the altar space, along with the Bible, to remind the family of their need for God's influence in their decisions about their country's political and economic issues.

Prayer: God of all creation, we thank you for the variety you have created, even in our family. We ask that our country might be a power for your goodness in the world. We offer ourselves to be channels of your truth. May you enlighten any dark or confused place in our minds. Amen.

Close: Share a hug with everyone, and enjoy the treat from your ancestral country.

Thirtieth Sunday in Ordinary Time

▪▪▪▪▪

"Teacher, which commandment of the law is the greatest?" Jesus said to him: "'You shall love the Lord your God with your whole heart, with your whole soul, and with all your mind.' This is the greatest commandment. The second is like it: 'You shall love your neighbor as yourself.' On these two commandments the whole law is based, and the prophets as well."

Materials: ✓ blue construction paper (from which you cut "1st Place" ribbons, enough for each person to have three or four) ✓ pens or pencils (one for each person)

Treat: ice cream or frozen yogurt (or banana splits, if you really want to celebrate)

Theme: We strive to love God with all we've got.

Reading: *Matthew 22:34-40 (Gospel)*
When the Pharisees heard that Jesus had silenced the Sadducees, they assembled in a body; and one of them, a lawyer, in an attempt to trip him up, asked him,

Leader's Instructions: Prepare the blue "1st Place" ribbons ahead of time. On each ribbon write, 1st PLACE—GOD. Gather the family, open with prayer, read the Scripture, place the ribbons in the center of the gathering, and lead the Share and Commit sections.

Share: Many times we focus on what we should do or change in ourselves. Today, our focus is on God. If Jesus says we are to love God completely, then there must be a reason. A young girl once asked why Saint Teresa of Avila loved God so much. Why? Because Saint Teresa was aware of how good God was to her.

How has God been good to you? Take a blue ribbon and write your responses on it.

Another time, Saint Teresa told God, "If this is the way you treat your friends, no wonder you have so few of them." Have there been times when you weren't sure if God was on your side? How did things turn out? If you were God, what would you do so that people would love you with all their hearts and minds and souls? What do you think we should do for ourselves to help us love God more and more?

Commit: Every morning, noon, and night this week, let's pause to think about the wonderful things God has done for us.

Altar Sign: Place the ribbons for God on the altar space, and let them serve as a reminder to thank God often.

Prayer: O mighty and good God, you love us and care for us. You focus your attention on us. We pray for the grace to remember your goodness and sweetness and to see the world with eyes of love. Amen.

Close: Give one another a hug from God, then enjoy the treat.

Thirty-First Sunday of Ordinary Time

Theme: We admire people for many reasons.

Reading: *Matthew 23:1-12 (Gospel)*
Jesus told the crowds and his disciples: "The scribes and the Pharisees have succeeded Moses as teachers; therefore, do everything and observe everything they tell you. But do not follow their example. Their words are bold but their deeds are few. They bind up heavy loads that are hard to carry on other people's shoulders, while they themselves will not lift a finger to budge them. All their works are performed to be seen. They widen their phylacteries and wear huge tassels. They are fond of places of honor at banquets and the front seats in synagogues, of marks of respect in public, and of being called 'Rabbi.' Only one among you is your teacher, the Messiah. The greatest among you will be the one who serves the rest. Those who exalt themselves shall be humbled, but those who humble themselves shall be exalted."

Materials: ✓ a dried chicken bone inside a beautifully wrapped box ✓ a plain empty box ✓ construction paper ✓ blank paper ✓ crayons ✓ pencils

Treat: Cracker Jacks™ or any snack with a prize inside

Leader's Instructions: Wrap the box with the chicken bone ahead of time. Gather the family, open with prayer, place the pretty box in the center of the gathering, read the Scripture, and lead the Share and Commit sections.

Share: Jesus warns the people and us today about being impressed by those who look good or holy. To get an idea of how this is, look at this pretty box: pretty paper, pretty bow. Now let's open it. (Ask one of the younger participants to unwrap the package and see what's inside.)

Sometimes those who spend all their time trying to impress others don't have much on the inside. Jesus tells us that truly great people are those who serve others. (Draw the group's attention to the plain box with the lid off.) Those people are filled with love of God, and their prayers and service might be hidden.

Who are the people that you think "have it all together"? What do they do that impresses you? Do you see yourself trying to be like them? Be wary of this because your focus shifts from God to them. When are you most concerned about impressing others? Do you ever find yourself jealous of others? How do you feel about yourself when you're trying to impress others? What do you think God would want you to remember at that time? (Ask someone to write or draw the responses to these questions on the plain paper. Put the paper in the plain box.)

Have you ever felt better after helping someone? Why do you think your feelings improve after you help others? How do you know when you have gotten overinvolved in helping others? Would Jesus approve if you had to say "No" sometimes when others ask for help? Why? Are there more people in the world who are "servers" or "self-exalters"? How can you tell which group you're in?

Commit: Several times this week, let's take the time to "rest in God," to let God love us as we are so we can be free of the need to impress others.

Altar Sign: Place the plain box on the altar space to remind family members not to exalt themselves.

Prayer: Dearest God, we seem to struggle so much with what others are thinking of us. We get so busy going places and doing things that do not make us happy. We pray for the grace to be satisfied in humble service to you. Amen.

Close: Offer a hug to each person, and say, "I love you as you are." Then share your treats.

Thirty-Second Sunday in Ordinary Time

Theme: We prepare to meet the Lord.

Reading: *Matthew 25:1-13 (Gospel)*
Jesus told this parable to his disciples: "The reign of God can be likened to ten bridesmaids who took their torches and went out to welcome the groom. Five of them were foolish, while the other five were sensible. The foolish ones, in taking their torches, brought no oil along, but the sensible ones took flasks of oil, as well as their torches.

"The groom delayed his coming, so they all began to nod, then to fall asleep. At midnight, someone shouted, 'The groom is here! Come out and greet him!' At the outcry, all the bridesmaids woke up and got their torches ready. The foolish ones said to the sensible, 'Give us some of your oil. Our torches are going out.' But the sensible ones replied, 'No, there may not be enough for you and us. You had better go to the dealers and buy yourselves some.'

"While they went off to buy it, the groom arrived, and the ones who were ready went into the wedding with him. Then the door was barred. Later, the other bridesmaids came back. 'Master, master!' they cried. 'Open the door for us.' But he answered, 'I tell you, I do not know you.' The moral is: keep your eyes open, for you know not the day or the hour."

Materials: ✓ a jump rope, weights, or some other exercise equipment

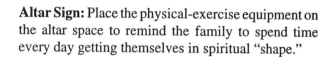

Treat: Jell-O,™ cut with cookie-cutter shapes

Leader's Instructions:

Gather the family, open with prayer, and place the equipment you've chosen inside the family circle. Read the Scripture, and lead the Share and Commit sections.

Share: We are familiar with getting our bodies in shape. This week's reading advises us to get our lives in shape for the coming of Christ.

Sometimes people wonder why the five bridesmaids wouldn't share just a little bit. But when it comes time to meet Christ, we won't be able to share even if we want to. Do you know why?

Some people take quiet time each night to review their feelings and actions of the day. How might this help prepare one for Christ? Some couples make a commitment to work out or talk out any angry feelings they have before going to sleep. How does this help them prepare to meet Christ?

What else might you do to "keep your eyes open"? How might receiving the sacraments prepare you?

Just as physical exercise is best when it is regular, so is spiritual exercise. What kind of regular spiritual exercise do you practice? If none, what might you start? Could you start daily prayer or Scripture reading? Would you like to go on a retreat? Would you like to connect with a spiritual director or prayer group? How could the family support you?

Commit: Each day this week, let's do some kind of spiritual exercise. Maybe we can begin a routine that will last a long time.

Altar Sign: Place the physical-exercise equipment on the altar space to remind the family to spend time every day getting themselves in spiritual "shape."

Prayer: God of heaven and earth, we thank you for making us in your image. We pray for the grace to be faithful to prayer, that we might become what we can be as your sons and daughters. Amen.

Close: Take a walk together, and enjoy your treat.

Thirty-Third Sunday in Ordinary Time

■ ■ ■ ■ ■ ■

Theme: We respect and use our abilities.

Reading: *Matthew 25:14-15, 19-26, 30 (Gospel)*
Jesus told this parable to his disciples: "A man going on a journey called in three servants and handed over to them an amount of funds according to each one's abilities. To one was distributed five thousand silver pieces, to a second two thousand, and to a third a thousand.

"After a long absence, the man came home and settled accounts with the servants. The one who had received the five thousand came forward bringing an additional five. 'Well done! You are an industrious and reliable servant. Since you were dependable in a small matter I will put you in charge of larger affairs.' The one who had received two thousand stepped forward with two thousand more. 'Cleverly done! You, too, are an industrious and reliable servant. Since you were dependable in a small matter, I will put you in charge of larger affairs.' Finally, the one who had received the thousand stepped forward. 'I knew you were a hard taskmaster. You reap where you did not sow and gather where you did not scatter, so out of fear I went off and buried your thousand silver pieces in the ground. Here is your money back.' 'You worthless, lazy lout! Throw this worthless servant into the darkness outside to wail and grind teeth.'"

Materials: ✓ rectangular papers, any color (five or six pieces for each person) ✓ pencils (one for each person)

PATIENT FUN HELPFUL

Treat: graham crackers, (with or without toppings of icing, nuts, coconut, raisins, cherries, whatever is desired)

Leader's Instructions: Prepare the rectangular pieces of paper ahead of time. For each member in the group, write an ability on one rectangle. The other rectangles will be used by the individuals themselves. The rectangles can be plain or bordered with "Better than gold" "In God we trust," or any other decoration that makes the paper look like "official" paper money. Gather the family, open with prayer, read the Scripture, and hand out the one ability paper you have written for each person. Lead the Share and Commit sections.

Share: No matter who we are, we have abilities. Jesus tells us it is not how much we have, but what we do with it, how we use it. To "bury" an ability means that we don't use it—and that's the worst thing we can do.

You have a sheet of paper with one of your abilities written on it. What other abilities do you think you have? How about other family members?

Do you think everyone in the family is using his or her abilities? Does fear keep people from using their abilities? It was fear that kept the servant in the parable from using his abilities. How could a person "bury" a talent? Why might someone do that?

How can we encourage one another to use their talents at home? at school? at work? in the neighborhood? at church? (Ask someone to write the responses on the remaining pieces of paper.)

Commit: This week, let's encourage one another to use our talents fully. Let's be open to using our talents as God desires.

Altar Sign: Place the ability papers on the altar space to remind the family that they have wonderful abilities and should use them well.

Prayer: God, giver of life and love, we thank you for the way you have blessed us with many abilities. May we use them for your glory and may we serve you each day. Amen.

Close: As you hug each family member, mention the ability you admire most in him or her. Share the treat, topping as each one desires.

Christ the King

......

Theme: Whatever we do to the least ones, we do to me.

Reading: *Matthew 25:31-46 (Gospel)*
Jesus said to his disciples: "When the Son of Man comes in his glory, escorted by all the angels of heaven, he will sit upon the royal throne, and all the nations will be assembled there. Then they will be separated into two groups, as a shepherd separates the sheep from goats. The sheep will be placed on the right and the goats on the left. Then, as king, he will say to those on his right: 'Come. You have God's blessing! Inherit the place prepared for you from the creation of the world. For I was hungry and you gave me food, I was thirsty and you gave me drink. I was a stranger and you welcomed me, naked and you clothed me. I was ill and you comforted me, in prison and you came to visit me.' Then the just will ask, 'When did we see you hungry and feed you or see you thirsty and give you drink? When did we welcome you away from home or clothe you in your nakedness? When did we visit you when you were ill or in prison?' The king will answer them: 'I assure you, as often as you did it for one of my least brothers or sisters, you did it for me.'

"Then he will say to those on the left: 'Out of my sight, you condemned, into that everlasting fire prepared for the devil and such angels! I was hungry and you gave me no food, I was thirsty and you gave me no drink. I was away from home and you gave me no welcome, naked and you gave me no clothing. I was ill and in prison and you did not come to comfort me.' They in turn will ask: 'When did we see you hungry or thirsty or away from home or naked or ill or in prison and not attend you in your needs?' The king will answer them: 'I assure you, as often as you neglected to do it to one of these least ones, you neglected to do it to me.' These will go off to eternal punishment and the just to eternal life."

Materials: ✓ pictures of friends or family members (or write the names of friends and family members on index cards) ✓ a big sheet of paper or poster board with a large question mark on it

Treat: raisins, red hots, or some other small-sized treat

Leader's Instructions: Gather the family, and open with prayer. Place the pictures or cards within the family circle, read the Scripture, and lead the Share and Commit sections.

Share: When one of these people (point to the pictures or index cards) is in need, we do all we can to help, just like the "sheep" in the reading. The question mark stands for all those other people who we don't know but do help, for those we avoid because of prejudices or fears, for those we turn away because we're worried what others will think of us if we help. But Jesus asks us to treat all people with love, kindness, and generosity.

Who might be some of the people you have helped and are helping without even realizing it? (Ask someone to write the responses on the paper or poster board with the question mark on it.) Who are people you don't even think about because they live far away or are shut away from your everyday life? (Ask someone to write the responses on the paper or poster board with the question mark on it.) Who are the kinds of people we would rather not bother with, associate with, or even talk with because we "hate" them, fear them, or don't feel anything at all toward them? (Ask someone to write the responses on the paper or poster board with the question mark on it.)

If Jesus were to separate the sheep and the goats today, which side do you think you'd be on? Why? Might members of the same family be on different sides? How, do you think, does Jesus take into account our various personalities and handicaps—or do you think all people could reach out to "the least"?

Think of one person or group of people on the question-mark card that you could help this week. Is there a way we can support you in this?

Commit: At least once this week, let's reach out to one of "the least" that Jesus talks about in the Scripture.

Altar Sign: Place the question-mark card on the altar space or tape it to the wall nearby to remind the family to reach out to those in need.

Prayer: Good God, you are fair and just. We pray for the grace to listen to Jesus' words with our hearts and will. May our eyes be opened to seeing those in need. May our hearts be opened to responding according to your will. Amen.

Close: Give all members a hug, and enjoy your treat.

THE SEASON OF
LENT

First Sunday of Lent

■■■■■

Theme: Faith is lived in the ordinary times of life.

Reading: *Matthew 4:1-11 (Gospel)*

Jesus was led into the desert by the Spirit to be tempted by the devil. He fasted forty days and forty nights, and afterward he was hungry. The tempter approached and said to him, "If you are the Son of God, command these stones to turn into bread." Jesus replied, "Scripture has it: 'Not on bread alone are we to live but on every utterance that comes from the mouth of God.'" Next, the devil took him to the Holy City, set him on the parapet of the temple, and said, "If you are the Son of God, throw yourself down. Scripture has it: 'God will bid the angels to take care of you; with their hands they will support you so that you may never stumble on a stone.'" Jesus answered, "Scripture also has it: 'You shall not put the Lord your God to the test.'" The devil then took him to a lofty mountain peak and displayed before him all the countries of the world in their magnificence, promising, "All of these I will bestow on you if you prostrate yourself in homage before me." At this, Jesus said to him, "Away with you, Satan! Scripture says: 'You shall do homage to the Lord your God, who alone shall you adore.'" At that the devil left him, and angels came and waited on him.

Materials: ✓ postcards of big cities or spectacular places (or pictures from a book or magazine) ✓ a picture of your house or a sheet of paper with your address written on it

Treat: plain toast (Have butter, jelly, marmalade, and other toppings available.)

Leader's Instructions: Gather the family, and open with prayer. Put the pictures and/or cards in the center of the group, read the Scripture, and lead the Share and Commit sections.

Share: In the reading, we hear about Jesus refusing the extraordinary, the spectacular. Sometimes there are boring or ordinary times in our lives; faith in Jesus and following Jesus does not mean it will always be exciting or spectacular.

Do you tend to get restless if nothing exciting is going on? Are you waiting for a miracle to truly give your heart to God? Are there some unspectacular things in your life you wish God would change? Do the unspectacular things cause you to doubt God's love for you just as you are, right now? How would you finish the sentence "I'll be okay when..."?

Does that give you a clue as to your dissatisfaction with the ordinary? What might you do instead? How can family members help you appreciate the ordinary and small wonders of life?

Commit: Each day this week, let's spend time noticing ordinary things: walking, baking, cleaning, talking, working. Let's be especially aware of how God loves us in those ordinary moments.

Altar Sign: Place the picture of your house or the card with your address on the altar space. Let it remind you to live and love in the ordinariness of life.

Prayer: God of day and night, summer and winter, season after season, we thank you for the routines of our lives that give stability. We ask your blessing on those times when we are restless. We pray for the grace to rest in you and your world. Amen.

Close: Hug each family member, and share the treat.

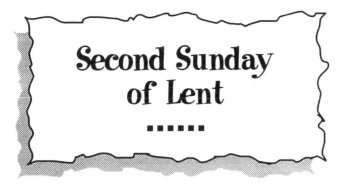

Second Sunday of Lent

Theme: God transfigures us.

Reading: *Matthew 17:1-3, 5-9 (Gospel)*
Jesus took Peter, James, and his brother John and led them up on a high mountain by themselves. He was transfigured before their eyes. His face became as dazzling as the sun, his clothes as radiant as light. Suddenly, Moses and Elijah appeared to them conversing with him and a bright cloud overshadowed them. Out of the cloud came a voice which said, "This is my beloved Son on whom my favor rests. Listen to him." When the disciples heard this, they fell forward on the ground, overcome with fear. Jesus came toward them and laying his hand on them, said, "Get up! Do not be afraid." When they looked up they did not see anyone but Jesus. As they were coming down the mountainside, Jesus commanded them, "Do not tell anyone of the vision until the Son of Man rises from the dead."

Materials: ✓ mirrors, small enough to be held in one's hand

Treat: nut bread

Leader's Instructions: Gather the family, and place the mirrors in the center of the group. Open with prayer. Before you read the Scripture, explain that last week's reading was about Jesus resisting temptation to do the spectacular. Remind the family that Jesus was content to trust God in the ordinary. Explain that this week's reading tells about the Transfiguration of Jesus—definitely spectacular! After you read the Scripture, lead the Share and Commit sections.

Share: When you look in the mirror at yourself, what is your first thought or reaction? Many people in our society believe that they are not good enough because they compare themselves to an ideal of looks or popularity or amount of money earned.

How do people who don't think they're good enough act? Would a person who felt secure in God's love behave differently? How?

Have you ever seen someone who was "transformed" because of love? How do we let others know that they are loved? Would you like the family to do something special that lets you know you are loved? What?

Commit: This week, let's smile at ourselves every time we look in a mirror. At that moment, let's thank God for loving us.

Altar Sign: Place one of the small hand-held mirrors on the altar space. Each time you pass it this week, pause and smile and know that God smiles with you.

Prayer: Dear God, your image of who we are and what we can be is sometimes hidden to us. We pray for the grace to see ourselves as you see us, that we might be secure as we do your work here on earth. Amen.

Close: Share a hug, and enjoy the treat.

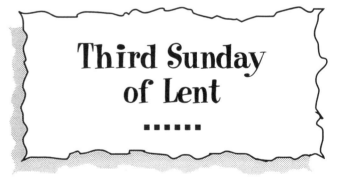

Third Sunday of Lent

Theme: Jesus desires to give eternal life.

Reading: *John 4:5-15, 19-26, 39, 40-42 (Gospel)*
Jesus had to pass through Samaria, and his journey

brought him to a Samaritan town named Sychar near the plot of land that Jacob had given to his son Joseph. This was the site of Jacob's well. Jesus, tired from his journey, sat down at the well. The hour was about noon.

When a Samaritan woman came to draw water, Jesus said to her, "Give me a drink." (His disciples had gone off into town to buy provisions.) The Samaritan woman said to him, "You are a Jew. How can you ask me, a Samaritan and a woman, for a drink?" (Recall that Jews have nothing to do with Samaritans.) Jesus replied: "If only you recognized God's gift, and who it is that is asking you for a drink, you would have asked him instead, and he would have given you living water." "Sir," she challenged him, "you don't have a bucket and this well is deep. Where do you expect to get this flowing water? Surely, you don't pretend to be greater than our ancestor Jacob, who gave us this well and drank from it with his family and flocks?" Jesus replied: "Everyone who drinks this water will be thirsty again. But whoever drinks the water I give will never be thirsty; no, the water I give shall become a fountain within, leaping up to provide eternal life."

The woman said to him, "Give me this water, sir, so that I won't grow thirsty and have to keep coming here to draw water. I can see you are a prophet. Our ancestors worshiped on this mountain, but you people claim that Jerusalem is the place where all ought to worship God." Jesus told her, "Believe me, woman, an hour is coming when you will worship God neither on this mountain nor in Jerusalem. An hour is coming, and is already here, when authentic worshipers will worship God in Spirit and truth. Indeed, it is just such worshipers that God seeks. God is Spirit, and those who worship must worship in Spirit and truth." The woman said to him: "I know there is a Messiah coming. When he comes, he will tell us everything." Jesus replied, "I who speak to you am he."

Many Samaritans from that town believed in him on the strength of the woman's word of testimony: "He told me everything I ever did." The result was that, when these Samaritans came to him, they begged him to stay with them awhile. So Jesus stayed there two days, and through his own spoken word many more came to faith. As they told the woman, "No longer does our faith depend on your story. We have heard for ourselves, and we know that this really is the Savior of the world."

Materials: ✓ See Appendix F on page 95 for characters in the story. Trace and cut out. (The family might enjoy coloring these ahead of time.) ✓ pencils ✓ scissors ✓ crayons or markers (optional)

Treat: gingerbread people, one per person

Leader's Instructions: Gather the family, and open with prayer. As you read the Scripture, have two or more people move the figures around to "act out" the story. Lead the Share and Commit sections.

Share: Which one of the characters in the story is spiritually like you? In what way? Have you been spiritually like one of the other people? Are you satisfied with how you "spiritually" are now? If you were at the well with Jesus today, what would you talk to him about? What do you think he would say to you?

Commit: This week, let's meet Jesus at the well in our imagination. Let's talk with him and listen to what he has to say to us.

Altar Sign: Place the figures from the story on the altar space as a reminder to talk to Jesus now, just as you are.

Prayer: Dear God, you are always willing to come and meet us where we are. We thank you for this and we pray for the grace to respond to you with our whole selves. Amen.

Close: Have a glass of water with your treat, and share a family hug.

Fourth Sunday of Lent

■ ■ ■ ■ ■

Theme: Seeing faith truths requires more than physical vision.

Reading: *John 9:1, 6-9, 13-17, 34-38 (Gospel)*
As Jesus walked along, he saw a man who had been blind from birth. With that, Jesus spat on the ground, made mud with his saliva, and smeared the man's eyes with the mud. Then Jesus told him, "Go wash in the pool of Siloam." So the man went off and washed and came back able to see. His neighbors and the people who had been accustomed to seeing him beg began to ask, "Isn't this the fellow who used to sit and beg?" Some were claiming it was he; others maintained it was not but someone who looked like him. The man himself said, "I'm the one, all right."

They took the man who had been born blind to the Pharisees. (Note that it was on a sabbath that Jesus had made the mud paste and opened his eyes.) The Pharisees, in turn, began to inquire how he had recovered his sight. He told them. "He put mud on my eyes. I washed it off, and now I can see." This prompted some of the Pharisees to assert, "This man cannot be from God because he does not keep the sabbath." Others objected, "If one is a sinner, how could that one perform signs like these?" They were sharply divided over him. Then they addressed the blind man again: "Since it was your eyes he opened, what do you have to say about him?" "He is a prophet," he replied. "What!" they exclaimed. "You are steeped in sin from your birth and you are giving us lectures?" With that, they threw him out bodily.

When Jesus heard of his expulsion, he sought him out and asked him, "Do you believe in the Son of Man?" He answered, "Who is he, sir, that I may believe in him?" "You have seen him," Jesus replied. "He is speaking to you now." "I do believe, Lord," he said, and bowed down to worship him.

Materials: ✓ three scarves or similar material (long enough to use as a blindfold)

Treat: a layered treat (for example, double-dip cone or sandwich cookies)

Leader's Instructions: Gather the family members, open with prayer, and ask for a volunteer to be blindfolded. Explain to the person that he or she will have to remain patient throughout the Scripture reading. Tie the scarves around the person's eyes, creating three layers of darkness. (Be sure the person can breathe.) Begin reading the Scripture. When you read the part about the man washing off the mud and being able to see, have someone remove the outermost scarf from the blindfolded person. When you read the part about the man stating that Jesus is a prophet, have someone remove the next scarf. When you read the final statement, "I do believe, Lord," have the final scarf removed. Lead the Share and Commit sections.

Share: Why didn't all three scarves come off when the blind man was able to see? What does this tell us about our faith life, even if we can see with our eyes? In what ways can we use all our senses and our other capabilities to increase our faith and that of others? How can we help one another do this?

Jesus broke the law of not working on the sabbath. When might it be okay to ignore a law as Jesus did?

Commit: This week, let's use one of our senses each day to increase our own faith or that of another person.

Altar Sign: Place the three scarves on the altar space to remind the family of the constant unwrapping that is involved in spiritual seeing and growing.

Prayer: O God, our creator, you made us with so much potential and with so many abilities. Help us use what we have in a way that increases our faith. We pray for the grace to know how you need us to do this. Amen.

Close: Share a hug and the treat.

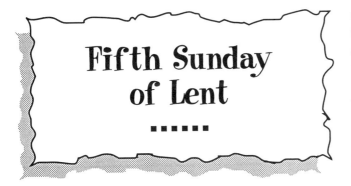

Fifth Sunday of Lent

■■■■■

Theme: Faith in Jesus unbinds us.

Reading: *John 11:3-7, 17, 20-27, 33-45 (Gospel)*
Two sisters sent word to Jesus to inform him, "Lord, the one you love is sick." Upon hearing this, Jesus said: "This sickness is not to end in death; rather it is for God's glory, that through it the Son of God may be glorified." Jesus loved Martha and her sister and Lazarus very much. Yet, after hearing that Lazarus was sick, he stayed on where he was for two days more. Finally, he said to his disciples, "Let us go back to Judea."

When Martha heard that Jesus was coming, she went to meet him, while Mary sat at home. Martha said to Jesus, "Lord, if you had been here, my brother would never have died. Even now, I am sure that God will give you whatever you ask." "Your bother will rise again," Jesus assured her. "I know he will rise again," Martha replied, "in the resurrection on the last day." Jesus told her, "I am the resurrection and the life: those who believe in me, though they die, will come to life; and those who are alive and believe in me will never die. Do you believe this?" "Yes, Lord," she replied. "I have come to believe that you are the Messiah, the Son of God: the one who is to come into the world."

When Jesus saw Mary weeping and the Jewish folk who had accompanied her out of the house also weeping, he was troubled in spirit, moved by the deepest emotions. "Where have you laid him?" Jesus asked. "Lord, come and see," they said. Jesus began to weep, which caused the Jews to remark, "See how much he loved him!" But some said, "He opened the eyes of that blind man. Why could he not have done something to stop this man from dying?"

Once again, troubled in spirit, Jesus approached the tomb. It was a cave with a stone laid across it. "Take away the stone," Jesus directed. Martha said to him, "Lord, it has been four days now; surely there will be a stench!" Jesus replied, "Did I not assure you that if you believed you would see the glory of God?" They then took away the stone, and Jesus looked upward and said, "Father, I thank you for having heard me. I know that you always hear me but I have said this for the sake of the crowd, that they may believe that you sent me." Having said this, he called loudly, "Lazarus, come out!" The dead man came out, bound hand and foot with linen strips, his face wrapped in a cloth. "Untie him," Jesus told them, "and let him go free." This caused many of the Jews who had come to visit Mary, and had seen what Jesus did, to put their faith in him.

Materials: ✓ 12- by 24-inch strips of cloth or gauze (one per person)

Treat: long strips of taffy or licorice

Leader's Instructions: Using the strips of cloth or gauze, wrap together all the fingers on each person's hands and/or wrap their legs together at the ankles. Do this twenty to thirty minutes before the meeting, and then ask the family to gather. After opening prayer, begin reading the Scripture. When you read the part about Jesus commanding Lazarus to be untied, direct family members to untie one another. Lead the Share and Commit sections.

Share: Why was it good for us to experience having our hands and feet tied? What are some ways people are not free within themselves?

What fears, worries, or memories keep you from being free to act as you believe Jesus would want you to act? How can we help one another attain freedom? If you have some hurt in your life about which, like Martha, you want to say to God, "If only you had...," would you be willing to forgive God and trust God again? How could someone help you do that?

Jesus said that he knew God always heard his prayers. How do you know when God has heard your prayers?

Commit: Every day this week, let's pray for the grace to be free of a particular worry, fear, or memory. Let's act on that as we feel led by God.

Altar Sign: Place the strips of cloth or gauze on the altar space to remind the family that they are set free by Christ. Encourage the family to pray by the altar space when they need the courage to be free from some fear.

Prayer: O God, your Son lived with us and knew how much we hurt. We pray that through him, you will set us free. We pray for the grace to be free and for the wisdom to know what to do. Amen.

Close: Share a hug and the treat.

Passion Sunday
(PALM SUNDAY)
■ ■ ■ ■ ■ ■

Theme: Popularity doesn't last; faithfulness to God does.

Reading: *Matthew 21:1-11*
(Gospel from the Procession)
As the crowd drew near Jerusalem, entering Bethphage on the Mount of Olives, Jesus sent off two disciples

with the instruction: "Go into the village straight ahead of you and you will immediately find an ass and her colt tied there. Untie them and lead them back to me. If anyone says a word to you say, 'The master needs them.' Then he will let them go at once." This came about to fulfill what was said through the prophet: "Tell the daughter of Zion, your king comes to you without display astride an ass, astride a colt, the foal of a beast of burden."

So the disciples went off and did what Jesus had ordered; they brought the ass and the colt and laid their cloaks on them, and he mounted. The huge crowd spread their cloaks on the road, while some began to cut branches from the trees and laid them along his path. The groups preceding him as well as those following kept crying out: "God save the Son of David! Blessed be he who comes in the name of God! God save him from on high!" As Jesus entered Jerusalem the whole city was stirred to its depths, demanding, "Who is this?" And the crowd kept answering, "This is the prophet Jesus from Nazareth in Galilee."

Materials: ✓ one balloon
✓ palm branches

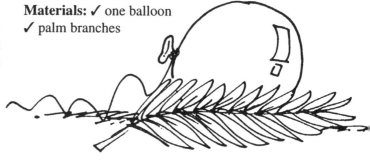

Treat: matzo crackers and apple slices

Leader's Instructions: Gather the family. After opening prayer, begin the reading. When you get to the part about the crowd cutting branches and crying out, blow up the balloon and tie it. As you finish the reading, hold the balloon and ask: "Will it stay blown up forever?" When someone responds "No," go on to explain that Jesus' popularity didn't last forever either. It was going to fade as people let themselves be pressured by some of the religious leaders and others around them. Then have the older children or other adults tell the story from the Last Supper to Jesus' burial, using the following events as guidelines: (1) the betrayer; (2) the Last Supper; (3) Peter's denial foretold; (4) the agony in the Garden; (5) Jesus arrested; (6) Jesus before the Sanhedrin; (7) Peter's denial; (8) Jesus handed over to Pilate; (9) Jesus before Pilate; (10) the crowning with thorns; (11) the way to the cross; (12) the Crucifixion; (13) the death of Jesus; (14) the burial of Jesus.

Share: How do you think the disciples of Jesus felt after the burial? We have the advantage today of knowing that he would rise again and is still with us. When you feel like the disciples did, for whatever reason, how will you remember that Jesus is risen and with you? What would you like the family to do for you at those times?

Have there been times when you were popular but lost that popularity? Looking back, do you notice a difference in your faith life during those times?

Commit: This week, let's support one another when we're feeling low. Let's be constant in faith despite rising or decreasing popularity. Let's attend services for the Easter Triduum—Holy Thursday, Good Friday, and Holy Saturday.

Altar Sign: Leave the balloon on the altar space as a reminder to be faithful to God no matter how popular it might or might not be.

Prayer: O God of heaven, you looked down and saw how people treated Jesus. We ask for the grace to be as faithful as he was when people mistreat us or misunderstand us. Amen.

Close: Share a hug, and enjoy your treat.

THE SEASON OF
EASTER

Easter Sunday
(EASTER VIGIL)
■ ■ ■ ■ ■

Theme: Some things are too good to be true!

Reading: *Matthew 28:1-10 (Gospel)*

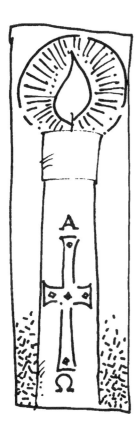

After the sabbath, as the first day of the week was dawning, Mary Magdalene and the other Mary came to see the tomb. And behold, there was a great earthquake; for an angel of the Lord descended from heaven, approached, rolled back the stone, and sat upon it. His appearance was like lightning and his clothing was white as snow. The guards were shaken with fear of him and became like the dead.

Then the angel said to the women in reply, "Do not be afraid! I know that you are seeking Jesus the crucified. He is not here, for he has been raised just as he said. Come and see the place where he lay. Then go quickly and tell the disciples, 'He has been raised from the dead, and he is going before you to Galilee; there you will see him.' Behold I have told you."

Then they went away quickly from the tomb, fearful yet overjoyed, and ran to announce this to the disciples. And behold, Jesus met them on their way and greeted them. They approached, embraced his feet, and did him homage. Then Jesus said to them, "Do not be afraid. Go tell my brothers and sisters to go to Galilee, and there they will see me."

Materials: ✓ white candle ✓ the word JOY cut out of white or yellow construction paper ✓ pencil ✓ dyed eggs (if your family does this tradition)

Treat: a family dessert that is extremely special

Leader's Instructions: Gather the family. Open with prayer, and read the Scripture. As you read the angel's words, "He has been raised from the dead," light the candle. Finish the reading, and lead the Share and Commit sections.

Share: Would you like to have been at the scene of the Resurrection? What would you have done, thought, or felt?

Have there been times when you felt so glad about something, you couldn't believe it? Did you ever think something was just too good to be true? (Ask someone to write the responses to these questions on the JOY letters.) What did you do with your gladness? How does it feel to remember it now? (Optional: How do these eggs we've dyed help us celebrate the joy of today?)

Commit: Let's take time each day this week to remember the joy of the people in the gospel and our joy at the "too-good-to-be-true" times. Let's remember this joy as we go about our days.

Altar Sign: Put the white candle on the altar space, and leave it there throughout the Easter season. Place the JOY letters next to it. (If you have dyed eggs, place them on the altar space as well.) Let the candle and the JOY letters remind you of the joy that is yours as you share in the victory of the risen Christ.

Prayer: God of joy and gladness, we thank you for the joy and life your Son, Jesus, has brought to us. We pray to live each day in that joy, no matter what might happen. We pray for the grace to bring joy to others. Amen.

Close: Hug one another, and enjoy your treat.

Second Sunday of Easter

■ ■ ■ ■ ■

Theme: Peace is tied to forgiveness.

Reading: *John 20:19-23 (Gospel)*

On the evening of that first day of the week, even though the disciples had locked the doors of the place

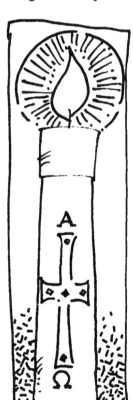

where they were for fear of the Jews, Jesus came and stood before them. "Peace be with you," he said. When he had said this, Jesus showed them his hands and his side. At the sight of the Lord, the disciples rejoiced. "Peace be with you," Jesus said again. "As the Father has sent me, so I send you." Then he breathed on them and said, "Receive the Holy Spirit. If you forgive sins, they are forgiven; if you hold them bound, they are held bound."

Materials: ✓ the white candle that's been on the altar space all week ✓ one index card with SORRY written on it ✓ one index card with I FORGIVE YOU written on it

Treat: any flavor of pie ("humble" pie)

Leader's Instructions: Gather the family, light the candle, and open with prayer. Read the Scripture, and lead the Share and Commit sections.

Share: Any peace that Jesus brings us is always influenced by our relationships with others. For that reason, we need to take some time to clear up any old or new wounds and go on in peace with one another. We'll use these index cards to help us.

Bow your head and close your eyes. Is there a person who has hurt your feelings? Are you angry or hurt? In yourself, prepare your heart to forgive this person. When you're ready, look at the person and tell him or her what it is that has hurt your feelings. That person should pick up the SORRY card, (if he or she is sorry) and the first person should pick up the I FORGIVE YOU card. If the second person does not happen to be sorry, the first can forgive anyway.

(After everyone has had a turn, continue.) How easy or hard was it to tell someone what he or she did that hurt your feelings? How did it feel to be told that you hurt someone's feelings? What patterns do you notice in what we've heard here today? What might we as a family do about it? How often do you think we should take the time to do this? How often should we celebrate the sacrament of reconciliation?

Commit: This week, let's ask for forgiveness as soon as we're aware that we've hurt someone's feelings. Let's be honest with one another, in the moment, about what's bothersome—before grudges build up.

Altar Sign: Put the candle back on the altar space, and place the two index cards against it. The candle and cards will remind the family that Christ is the source of the desire to forgive and the power to be healed.

Prayer: Dear God, you are the expert at forgiving and letting people start over again with no hard feelings. We ask for your help in doing this in our family. May we feel the rewards of peace. Amen.

Close: Give one another a hug, and eat your pie.

Third Sunday of Easter

■ ■ ■ ■ ■ ■

Theme: We don't want to become so "wrapped up" in our own ideas and fail to recognize God's work.

Reading: *Luke 24:13-35 (Gospel)*
That same day, two disciples of Jesus were making their way to a village named Emmaus, seven miles distant from Jerusalem, discussing as they went all that had happened. In the course of their lively exchange, Jesus approached and began to walk along with them. However, they were restrained from recognizing him. He said to them, "What are you discussing as you go your way?" They halted in distress, and one of them, Cleopas by name, asked him, "Are you the only resident of Jerusalem who does not know the things that went on there these past few days?" He said to them, "What things?" They said, "All those things that had to do with Jesus of Nazareth, a prophet powerful in word and deed in the eyes of God and all the people; how our chief priests and leaders delivered him up

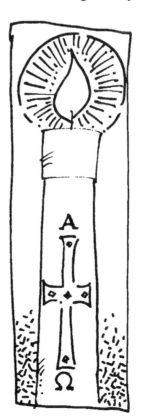

to be condemned to death and crucified him. We were hoping that he was the one who would set Israel free. Besides all this, today, the third day since these things happened, some women of our group have just brought us some astonishing news. They were at the tomb before dawn and failed to find his body, but returned with the tale that they had seen a vision of angels who declared he was alive. Some of our number went to the tomb and found it to be just as the women said; but they did not see him."

Then Jesus said the them, "What little sense you have! How slow you are to believe all that the prophets have announced! Did not the Messiah have to undergo all this so as to enter into his glory?"

Beginning, then, with Moses and all the prophets, he interpreted for them every passage of Scripture that referred to him. By now they were near the village to which they were going, and he acted as if he were going farther. But they pressed him: "Stay with us. It is nearly evening—the day is practically over." So he went in to stay with them. When he had seated himself with them to eat, he took bread, pronounced the blessing, then broke the bread and began to distribute it to them. With that, their eyes were opened and they recognized him; whereupon he vanished from their sight. They said to one another, "Were not our hearts burning inside us as he talked to us on the road and explained the Scriptures to us?" They got up immediately and returned to Jerusalem, where they found the eleven and the rest of the company assembled. They were greeted with "The Lord has been raised! It is true! He has appeared to Simon." Then they recounted what had happened on the road and how they had come to know him in the breaking of the bread.

Materials: ✓ the white candle that's been on the altar all week ✓ two figures (could be some dolls or action toys) ✓ two small pieces of paper to wrap around the figures (2 by 4 inches long) ✓ tape ✓ pencils ✓ picture or statue of Jesus

Many times we decide for ourselves how we want something to work out. Then, when it doesn't work that way, we're "stumped." Most of the disciples were like this, and it prevented them from recognizing God working even in the things they thought were terrible.

When have things gone differently than you planned with friendships? at school? at work? with family relationships? How did you react? Do you remember wondering where God was? Was it possible for you to say to God, "I don't know what you are doing, but I still am open to trusting you?"

Are there some areas of our lives in which we are willing to be open and other areas in which we're not? Why is there a difference? (Ask someone to write these responses on the paper that was wrapped around the figures.)

Commit: This week, let's be willing to open ourselves and our lives to what God needs from us rather than insisting on our own way.

Treat: wrapped candies (sugar-free or with sugar, as desired)

Leader's Instructions: This reading is long, but if you tell it as a story and let others add interest to the story by moving the figures and picture, younger children shouldn't be lost. Wrap the paper around the figures before the meeting, and hold the paper in place with tape. When you read the Scripture, leave the "wrappings" on until the part, "with that their eyes were opened." At that point, lay the paper flat (to use during the Share section).

Gather the family, light the candle, open with prayer, read the Scripture, and lead the Share and Commit sections.

Share: Do you think you would have recognized Jesus if you had been on the road to Emmaus that day? Why were the couple in the gospel not expecting Jesus to be risen?

Altar Sign: Place the candle and the wrappers from the figures on the altar space to remind the family to trust God and let God's plan unfold.

Prayer: God, you know our hopes and dreams. Sometimes we worry about letting go of them, but we know we must in order to be open to what you need. We pray for the grace to trust in you, to offer you all we have and possess, that you might use it according to your holy will. Amen.

Close: Share a hug, and enjoy the treat.

Fourth Sunday of Easter

■ ■ ■ ■ ■

Theme: The Lord is our protector and guide.

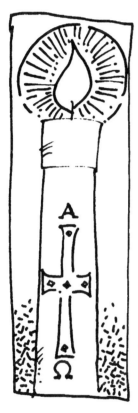

Reading: *Psalm 23 (Responsorial Psalm)*

The Lord is my shepherd; I shall not want. In verdant pastures he gives me repose; beside restful waters he leads me; he refreshes my soul. He guides me in right paths for his name's sake. Even though I walk in the dark valley, I fear no evil; for you are at my side with your rod and your staff that gives me courage. You spread the table before me in the sight of my foes; you anoint my head with oil; my cup overflows. Only goodness and kindness follow me all the days of my life; and I shall dwell in the house of the Lord for years to come.

Materials: ✓ the white candle that's been on the altar space all week ✓ paper ✓ pencils

✓ tape player and tape (optional)

Treat: a refreshing drink (fruit and ice blended together)

Leader's Instructions: Gather the family, light the candle, and start with opening prayer. Read the Scripture, and lead the Share and Commit sections.

Share: Not too many of us are around shepherds and sheep these days, but in Jesus' time it was quite common. Different images today can still give a message of protection, guidance, and the other themes in the Twenty-third Psalm. Sometimes putting something in our own words helps us understand it better. Let's try to do that with the psalm.

What do you think of when each line of the psalm is read? What feelings are expressed in the psalm? Write these down. (People can work individually, in pairs, or as one group.) What images—people, animals, things—from today help get across those same thoughts and feelings? Working with those feelings and images, write another version of the Twenty-third Psalm. (Everyone might want to try putting his or her version to a "rap" beat, a popular song, or a "golden-oldie" song. Share every version of the psalm that has been written by individuals, pairs, or the group. If a version has been put to music, record it.)

Which version do you like the best? Why? What did you learn about how you and others feel about Jesus? What surprised you about this project? Could we do something similar with other psalms, like Psalm 22, 54, 62, or 141?

Commit: This week, let's make at least one other psalm our own to help us pray.

Altar Sign: Place the candle and the family versions of the Twenty-third Psalm on the altar as a celebration of your experiences of God's protection and guidance.

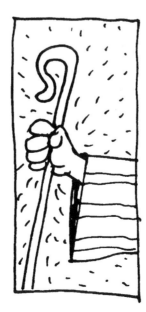

Prayer: Dear God, since before Jesus came to live on earth, people have looked to you and prayed to you for protection and guidance. May we always remember to do so, never losing hope in your goodness and love. Amen.

Close: Give one another a hug, and enjoy the treat.

Fifth Sunday of Easter

......

Theme: Jesus leads us to an understanding of God.

Reading: *John 14:1,3-11 (Gospel)*
Jesus said to his disciples, "Do not let your hearts be troubled. Have faith in God and faith in me. I am going to prepare a place for you, and then I shall come back to take you with me, that where I am you also may be. You know the way that leads where I go."

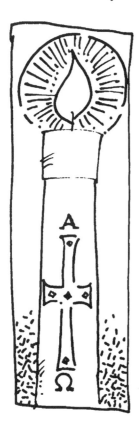

"Lord," said Thomas, "we do not know where you are going. How can we know the way?" Jesus told him, "I am the way, and the truth, and the life; no one comes to God but through me. If you really knew me, you would know my Father also. From this point on you know God; you have seen God."

"Lord," Philip said to him, "show us God and that will be enough for us." "Philip," Jesus replied, "after I have been with you all this time, you still do not know me? Whoever has seen me has seen God. How can you say, 'Show us God?' Do you not believe that I am in God and God is in me? The words I speak are not spoken of myself; it is the Father who lives in me accomplishing these works. Believe me that I am in God and God is in me, or else, believe because of the works I do."

Materials: ✓ the white candle that's been on the altar space all week ✓ sandpaper (a quarter or half sheet per person) ✓ crayons ✓ pieces of solid-color cloth (slightly larger than the pieces of sandpaper, one per person) ✓ an iron ✓ pencils

Treat: popcorn
(that our understanding might burst open in love of God)

Leader's Instructions: Gather the family, and light the candle. After opening prayer, read the Scripture, and lead the Share and Commit sections.

Share: Our understanding of Jesus leads us to understand God, yet of course, neither understanding is complete and we will hopefully continue to grow in knowing, loving, and serving God.

(Pass around all the materials.)

Think about symbols or images that represent what Jesus means to you. Draw and color that symbol or image on the rough side of the sandpaper. (When ironed onto the cloth, the image will be reversed; remember that if words are being used. As each person finishes drawing his or her image, have an adult place a piece of the cloth on the colored sandpaper. With the iron set on "wool," press down on the cloth until the colors transfer on the underside of the cloth. At a later date, someone might want to stitch all the pieces of cloth into a quilt.)

If you haven't already, explain your symbol. How has your understanding of God or your belief in God changed since you were younger? Do you know why it changed? What experiences might have caused it to change? Is there something about Jesus or God our creator/father that you would like to understand better? How might you go about gaining this understanding?

Commit: This week, notice what reminds you of God or Jesus. Let's begin to try to understand God or Jesus better in some way.

Altar Sign: Place the candle on the altar space, and hang the symbols on the wall nearby. Enjoy the beauty your family shows in their understanding of God.

Prayer: God, who gave us Jesus as part of you revealing yourself to us, we thank you. We ask that our knowledge of you might make us more in love with you. We pray for the grace to continue on this journey of knowledge, love, and service. Amen.

Close: Admire one another's images on the cloth, share a hug, and enjoy the treat.

Sixth Sunday of Easter

......

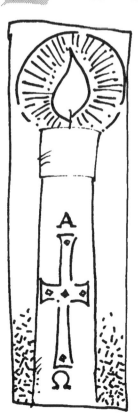

Theme: The Spirit of truth is not accepted by the world.

Reading: *John 14:15-18 (Gospel)*
Jesus said to his disciples, "If you love me and obey the commands I give you, I will ask the Father who will give you another Paraclete—to be with you always: the Spirit of truth, whom the world cannot accept, since it neither sees nor recognizes the Spirit; but you can recognize the Spirit because the Spirit remains with you and will be within you. I will not leave you orphaned; I will come back to you."

Materials: ✓ the white candle that's been on the altar space all week ✓ newspapers or magazines ✓ blank paper ✓ pencils ✓ ruler (optional)

Treat: peppermints

Leader's Instructions: Gather the family, light the candle, begin with opening prayer, and read the Scripture. Pass around the newspaper and/or magazines. Lead the Share and Commit sections.

Share: Look through the newspapers and/or magazines to find indications that the world has not seen, recognized, or accepted the Spirit of truth.

Do the news items or other items you see surprise you? How do you feel when you read these things? Do these news items show a world that takes the Spirit seriously? How could a person who listens to the Spirit expect to be treated in such a world? What kinds of items would be reported if the world did pay attention to the Spirit?

On the blank paper, make your own "Good News" sheet by adapting the stories you see in the papers and/or magazines—or make up your own story.

The fact that we can recognize the worldly verses the truth means the Spirit is within us. How can we encourage the growth of the Spirit of truth within us? In what ways might the family help us?

Commit: This week, let's oppose one thing that is presented as the "truth" when in actuality it is based on selfishness or lies. Let's help one another better recognize the Spirit of truth.

Altar Sign: Place the candle on the altar space, and tape the "Good News" sheet on the wall nearby to remind the family to look for the good and for the truth in the world.

Prayer: Dear God, the Spirit you have given us encourages us and calls us to greater holiness and purity. We pray for the grace to respond in courage and faithfulness. Amen.

Close: Share a hug, and enjoy the treat.

Seventh Sunday of Easter

Theme: We give God glory.

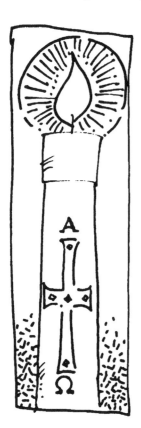

Reading: *John 17:1-11 (Gospel)*

Jesus looked up to heaven and said: "Father, the hour has come! Give glory to your Son that your Son may give glory to you, inasmuch as you have given him authority over all humanity, that he may bestow eternal life on those you gave him. I have given you glory on earth by finishing the work you gave me to do. Father, give me glory at your side, a glory I had with you before the world began. I have made your name known to those you gave me out of the world. These you gave me were yours, they have kept your word. Now they realize that all that you gave me comes from you. I entrusted to them the message you entrusted to me, and they received it. They have known that in truth I came from you, they have believed it was you who sent me. For these I pray—not for the world but for these you have given me, for they are really yours. It is in them that I have been glorified. I am in the world no more, but these are in the world as I come to you."

Materials: ✓ the candle that's been on the altar space all week ✓ a family portrait ✓ blank papers ✓ crayons ✓ pencils

Treat: peanut brittle

Leader's Instructions: Gather the family, and open with prayer. Remind those gathered that last week's focus was on the power of the Spirit and what a Spirit-led world might be like. Explain that this week's Scripture reminds us that God depends on us to bring the Good News to the world. After you read the Scripture, lead the Share and Commit sections.

Share: How does it feel to know that Jesus has entrusted his message to us? How does it feel to know that Jesus prayed for us? How could we, as a family, be a stronger force in the world than just one of us alone? How can we, as a family, bring Jesus' message to the world? (Ask if anyone would like to draw a picture that represents the family bringing the Good News to the world.)

Commit: This week, let's pray for our family as Good News bearers to the world. Let's ask God to grace us with the courage and strength we need.

Altar Sign: Place on the altar the candle, the family portrait, and the picture(s) representing the family bringing the Good News to the world. Let these items remind you—as a family—to work for God.

Prayer: Dearest God, you gave your Son to the world so that we might know you fully and share eternal life with you. We pray for the grace to continue in that work. We offer ourselves to be used in any way you need us. Amen.

Close: Share a family hug, and enjoy the treat.

Pentecost

■ ■ ■ ■ ■

Materials: ✓ the white candle that's been on the altar space all week ✓ pizza dough in a pan (If you don't have the time or energy to make dough, use canned biscuits, flattened out.) ✓ tomato sauce ✓ a variety of toppings ✓ index cards ✓ pens or pencils (optional)

Treat:
a pizza with a variety of toppings

Leader's Instructions: Gather the family, light the candle, and open with prayer. Place the pan of pizza dough, tomato sauce, and toppings within the family circle. Lead the Share and Commit sections.

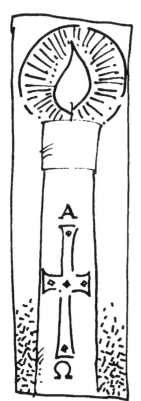

Theme: The Spirit is given for the good of all.

Reading: *1 Corinthians 12:3-7, 12-13 (Reading II)*
No one can say: "Jesus is Lord," except in the Holy Spirit. There are different gifts but the same Spirit; there are different ministries but the same Lord; there are different works but the same God, who accomplishes all of them in everyone. To each person the manifestation of the Spirit is given for the common good. The body is one and has many members, but all the members, many though they are, are one body; and so it is with Christ. It was in one Spirit that all of us, whether Jew or Greek, slave or free, were baptized into one body. All of us have been given to drink of the one Spirit.

Share: Pentecost is the day we celebrate the coming of the Holy Spirit upon the early leaders of the Church. It was a time when many wonderful gifts were poured out in the Church. This outpouring has not stopped. People all over the world, us included, are moved by the Spirit to do good works for the benefit of the "common good"—which is our own family, our neighbors, our town (city), the Church, or the world. We are unique in the gifts that we have and in the way we express them, but all of our gifts help to build up the Body of Christ. This is not something we need to be vain about, for it is God who is accomplishing this in us; it is God who has gifted us in the first place.

Let's take a few moments to recall the good works we've done lately. Each time we remember a good work, let's mention it, decorate the pizza by adding a topping, and say, "Thank you, God, for your gift to us." (Since this is the birthday of the Church, we will celebrate with pizza instead of a birthday cake.)

When have you helped another get closer to God by giving advice? When have you helped someone understand Scripture or life by sharing knowledge or teaching? When have you encouraged someone? When have you helped to heal another—physically, emotionally, or spiritually? When have you spoken out about the right thing to do? When have you helped someone figure out what was right or wrong? When have you prayed for another? All of these are gifts of the Spirit.

Let's rejoice and enjoy the "fruit" of our works! (Put the pizza in the oven to cook while you continue.)

Commit: This week, let's look for opportunities to give any of these gifts. Let's pray for the Spirit to be released in our world, in all people. (You might want to write on an index card the gift that each person would like increased in him or her.)

Altar Sign: Place the candle and the washed empty pizza pan on the altar space as signs of the joy that will be yours because of God "using" you to accomplish good things. (If you wrote "gifts" on index cards, tape them to the pizza pan.)

Prayer: Dear God in heaven, we thank you for the gift of your Spirit, who has in turn gifted us. May we be united in our efforts to build up your body here on earth. We pray for the grace to be open to the Spirit moving within us. Amen.

Close: Cut the pizza, and enjoy it!

APPENDICES

Appendix A

■■■■■

LITURGICAL SEASONS

Season	Color	
Advent	Blue	Begins four weeks before Christmas
Christmas	White	Begins with Christmas and concludes with Baptism of the Lord
Ordinary Time	Green	Begins the week after the Baptism of the Lord and is suspended during the season of Lent
Lent	Purple	Begins six weeks prior to Easter
Easter	White	Begins with Easter Sunday and concludes with Pentecost
Ordinary Time	Green	Begins again with Trinity Sunday and continues through the feast of Christ the King

Appendix B

■■■■■

DOVE
(For use with Baptism of the Lord)

Materials: ✓ piece of white poster board, 8 inches by 6 inches ✓ plain white paper or white tissue paper, 4 inches square ✓ glue ✓ pencils ✓ three pieces of white ribbon 6 to 8 inches long (optional)

Trace the figure below onto a piece of white poster board or white construction paper. Be sure to include the wing line: the small inside line that indicates where the wings will be inserted.

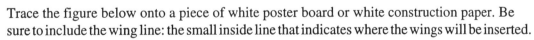

Cut the figure out of the white poster board or white construction paper. Cut along the wing line.

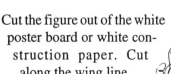

Accordion-pleat the plain white paper diagonally. Put it in the slit made for the wings, then open each end of the folded paper.

If using the ribbons, curl them by pulling them tightly over the blade of a scissor. Glue them in place for tail feathers.

Appendix C

FACE-VASE FIGURE
(For use with the Fourth Sunday in Ordinary Time)

Appendix D

......

PAPER FOLDING MAGIC
(For use with Trinity Sunday)

Materials: ✓a tracing of the figure provided ✓ scissors ✓ tape

Cut out the figure, cutting along solid lines only. The dotted lines are for folding only.

1. Crease all dotted lines.

2. Fold flaps A and B underneath.

3. Lift points C and D toward each other.

4. Tape E to F and G to H.

Amaze your family when you tell them it is made from one piece of paper!

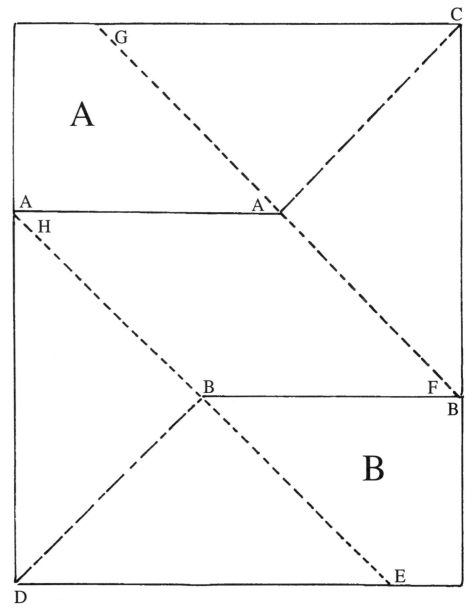

Appendix E

■ ■ ■ ■ ■ ■

PAPER BLOWERS
(For use with the Tenth Sunday in Ordinary Time)

Materials: ✓ one piece of notebook-size paper per blower (Tissue paper works best.)

Fold the paper one inch on the side, then continue folding over and over until it is all folded. You should have a strip one inch wide and as long as the paper.

Fold one end up about an eighth of an inch and crease it firmly.

Roll the strip around the creased fold to two inches from the end.

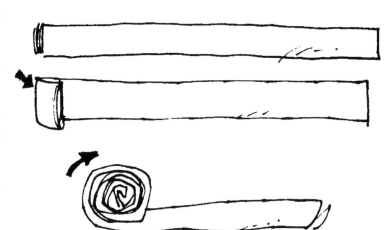

The unrolled end should form a hollow tube. Blow into it and let go of the rolled end. The blower will straighten out.

For more blowing fun, just reroll the blower, and repeat the process.

Appendix F

■■■■■

CHARACTERS FOR THE STORY OF THE WOMAN AT THE WELL
(For use with the Third Sunday in Lent)

Materials: ✓ stiff construction paper or poster board ✓ crayons or markers ✓ pieces of clay

Trace the outlines of the figures onto stiff construction paper or poster board. Cut them out and color the figures as you like, or let family members color them before the Scripture reading. In order to move them around easily during the reading, place the bottom of each figure in a one-inch ball of clay, flattened at the bottom.

Jesus

Disciples

Samaritan woman

Samaritan townspeople